The Second Half of Marriage

LEADER'S GUIDE

RESOURCES BY DAVID AND CLAUDIA ARP

Books

10 Great Dates
Love Life for Parents
The Second Half of Marriage
Suddenly They're 13!
Quiet Whispers from God's Heart for Couples
Marriage Moments
Family Moments

Video Curriculum

10 Great Dates
The Second Half of Marriage
PEP (Parents Encouraging Parents) Groups for Moms
PEP Groups for Parents of Teens

For more information about these and other Marriage Alive Resources contact:

Marriage Alive International, Inc.
10028 Quarry Hill Place
Denver, CO 80134
Phone: 303.840.1518
Resource Line: 1.888.690.6667
Email: mailine97@aol.com
Website: www.marriagealive.com

The Second Half

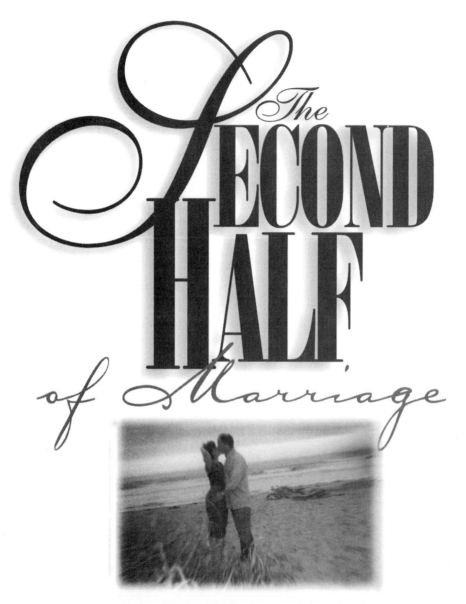

of Marriage

FACING THE EIGHT CHALLENGES
OF THE EMPTY-NEST YEARS

WRITTEN BY

DAVID & CLAUDIA ARP

WITH SHARON LAMSON

ZondervanPublishingHouse

Grand Rapids, Michigan

A Division of HarperCollinsPublishers

The Second Half of Marriage Leader's Guide
Copyright © 2000 by David and Claudia Arp

Requests for information should be addressed to:
ZondervanPublishingHouse
Grand Rapids, Michigan 49530

ISBN 0-310-23687-8

Published in association with the literary agency of Alive Communications, Inc., 7680 Goddard Street, Suite 200, Colorado Springs, CO 80920.

Interior design by Amy Langeler
Printed in the United States of America

00 01 02 03 04 05 06 /❖ PC/ 10 9 8 7 6 5 4 3 2 1

Contents

Introduction

For Claudia and Dave Arp, being the parents of three boys was both challenging and fun. They say that "with a few good parenting principles, lots of laughter, God's grace, and over twenty years of forced labor, we survived."

When the last child went off to college, the Arps discovered life after children! What would it hold for them? How would they manage their newfound "freedom"? Now they were in control of their home, schedules, and personal lives—or so they thought!

"It didn't take long to realize we had some work to do on our marriage," they write. "Our roles and responsibilities were turned upside down."

After searching for resources that could help them transition into this new stage of marriage, they were surprised to find very little practical material addressing the specific issues they faced. Being marriage educators and writers, they decided to take up the challenge and do the research themselves, so they conducted a national survey.

The Arps' research revealed eight challenges that all marriages face in the second half of life. With these eight challenges as a foundation, the Arps wrote the book *The Second Half of Marriage* and designed a seminar for empty nesters, to complement their popular Marriage Alive seminar. They then developed this video curriculum, which is based on their book and seminar, for you to use in leading your group. Unlike most marriage curricula, which focuses on the early years of marriage, this study addresses the unique challenges of marriage in midlife and beyond.

Since nothing is quite as helpful as real-life experience, the Arps have liberally sprinkled stories of their own marital struggles—as well as helpful tips from survey and seminar participants—throughout the book and video sessions.

This course is designed for those in midlife and beyond who want to deepen their relationship with their spouse. It's also appropriate for those who are in the second half of life but are in a new marriage. Wherever you are, according to the Arps, "you can make the rest the best!"

ABOUT THE AUTHORS

Dave and Claudia Arp are the founders and directors of Marriage Alive International, a groundbreaking ministry dedicated to providing resources and training to empower churches and others to help build stronger marriages and families. Their Marriage Alive seminar is popular both in the United States and in Europe. They are popular speakers, seminar leaders, columnists, and authors of numerous video curricula and books, including *10 Great Dates*, *Suddenly They're Thirteen*, and *Love Life for Parents*.

Frequent contributors to print and broadcast media, the Arps have appeared as empty nest experts on national programs such as the NBC *Today Show* and CBS *This Morning*. Their syndicated radio program, *The Family Workshop*, is heard daily on more than two hundred stations. Dave and Claudia have been married for over thirty-five years and live in Knoxville, Tennessee. They have three married sons and five grandchildren, so they have personally experienced what they share in this study. If you would like to know more about the Arps, their seminar schedule, or Marriage Alive, you can visit their web site at www.marriagealive.com.

ABOUT THIS COURSE—WHAT IT IS AND WHAT IT ISN'T

This is a ten-session marriage education course especially crafted for those in or near the empty nest years and on through the retirement years who want to deepen their relationship with their spouse and develop the skills they need to maintain a successful long-term marriage. The sessions and exercises are designed to guide couples to engage in meaningful dialogue about their own marriage, set goals, periodically evaluate their progress, and address issues that most couples will face at this stage of life.

This course is not designed to answer every specific question or address individual marital issues. Instead, participants will learn skills that will help them develop their own coping system. You will likely have couples who experience some marital dissatisfaction. Indeed, you may have couples whose marriages are in serious trouble. While this course can help point them in the right direction, it is not to be used in place of counseling. When deep problems exist, encourage participants to seek the help of their pastor or a professional counselor.

A FEW CHANGES

In the original format of *The Second Half of Marriage*, there was a discussion guide located at the back of the book, where the Participant's Guide is now located. Claudia and Dave refer to it during their "Message to Leaders" portion of the video. This Leader's Guide has been revised from the original to successfully guide you through leading the course.

BEFORE YOU START

Take a few moments to listen to the first two parts of video 1. The Arps have prepared some helpful statements for you in their "Message to Leaders." This segment of the tape is approximately four minutes long.

Then stay tuned for the "Short Preview." This three-minute segment can be used as a promotional tool for the course. A few weeks beforehand, invite couples who may be interested in enriching their marriage to watch the "Short Preview" and to sign up for the course. Set a date for when session 1 will begin, order your materials, and begin to prepare yourself to be an effective leader.

INCLUDED WITH THIS KIT

In this kit you should have the following:

- *The Second Half of Marriage Participant's Guide*
- Two one-hour videotapes
- A Leader's Guide that contains the text of the Participant's Guide found in the back of *The Second Half of Marriage Participant's Guide*

(Note: The trade book *The Second Half of Marriage*, which contains a discussion guide for use without the video curriculum, is not in this kit but is available at your local bookstore.)

OTHER TOOLS YOU WILL NEED

- For each participant, a copy of *The Second Half of Marriage Participant's Guide*. This Participant's Guide contains the text from the book *The Second Half of Marriage*, with a special Participant's Guide in the back of the book (these are specially marked editions).
- Videotape player
- Monitor with sound system
- Name tags
- Bible
- Pens and pencils for those who need them

HOW TO USE THIS LEADER'S GUIDE

The Leader's Guide is designed to help you be a successful facilitator. To further assist you, several typographical elements have been included.

- Text that is contained within a shaded box is instruction for you. These items are not meant to be read aloud to the group.
- Italicized text, such as in opening or closing prayers, is included as a suggestion. You may choose to read these items verbatim, or you may want to do something entirely different.
- Plain text should be read verbatim or paraphrased to fit your own personal style. These items include instructions to your group, introductions to the video clips, and questions for large-group discussion ("Marriage Forum"), small-group discussion ("One on One"), or individual exercises ("My Reflection Time").

Before the Session

Prior to class time, the leader should (1) read the "Leader Preparation," which summarizes the section or sections in the book that will be covered, (2) view the portion of the videotape that pertains to the class, and (3) go over the material in the Leader's Guide, making any necessary notes.

To gain a more in-depth knowledge of the material that is going to be covered, the leader is encouraged to read the corresponding chapters from the book *The Second Half of Marriage* before the class.

Participant's Guide

To eliminate the need for you to have a separate Participant's Guide, and to help you see how the material you are covering correlates to what your class members are seeing, a reduced-size copy of the Participant's Guide pages is included on the right-hand side of your Leader's Guide. Space is provided for the leader to make notes in preparation for leading the class.

SESSION FORMAT

The sessions are formatted in a way that will keep the class time flowing. Each segment is given an approximate time frame in which to complete the activities. This will help you keep your class on track and on time. Each session is divided into the following parts:

- Welcome
- Opening prayer
- Review of previous session
- Current session overview
- Video clip (except for session 10)
- "Marriage Forum" (large group discussion)
- "One on One" (time for couples to share privately)
- "My Reflection Time" (individual time to complete exercises)
- Wrap-up and closing prayer

A WORD ABOUT GROUP DISCUSSIONS

Groups of any size can present unique challenges to those who facilitate discussion. Because group dynamics vary, there are no specific guidelines that will work as a magic formula for each group. But there are some general principles you can apply to help your group run smoothly.

Usually groups consist of some basic types of people: those who like the limelight, the behind-the-scenes people, those who enjoy taking the opposite point of view, and people who never say anything. Each person is important to your group, and each type of personality brings a special flavor to group dynamics—it's all in how you, as the leader, apply the right guidance to bring about optimal results.

Those Who Like the Limelight

What group would be complete without those bold, sometimes dramatic individuals who just enjoy spontaneously talking? Often they express strong opinions. Many times these people have stories to tell that may or may not relate to the topic of discussion. These people are uncomfortable with periods of silence, so they fill it up. Sometimes they do so because they don't want the leader to look bad. There are all kinds of reasons why these people are the first (and often the last) to speak up.

Your group would probably be pretty quiet without these individuals, so you do not want to discourage their participation. Yet without some controls they could monopolize the discussion and even get it off track. Below are some points to consider in maximizing the valuable input these people have to offer, while at the same time minimizing their tendency to take over a discussion.

- Allow the person to speak as long as he stays on the subject. When you perceive that he is rambling or veering off track, interrupt him with something like, "Thank you, John, for some valuable insights, but I think we're getting a little off the subject. Does someone else have something to add to what John has just said?"
- When you ask the group a question, try to make eye contact with someone other than the people who tend to speak up frequently. That way you can direct the question to someone specifically.
- If someone repeatedly answers questions or makes remarks, you may have to privately speak to that person. Always affirm her for participating, but explain that you are trying to solicit response from people who never talk. Let her know that you expect and are okay with silent spots in the discussion. Ask her to help you generate greater group participation by refraining from answering as many questions. Also let her know that you will call upon her specifically to respond to certain questions to which you believe she would have good input.

The Behind-the-Scenes People

There are wonderful people who don't like to be onstage but love to be in the hub of backstage activity. Whether it's painting the set, designing the costumes, writing the script, or directing the play, they are in their element as long as they don't have to perform.

These personalities react the same way in group discussion. They may prod someone else to respond or they may write letters afterward expressing their opinion, but they are extremely uncomfortable speaking in front of a large group of people—and the term "large group" is personally defined. Yet these individuals often have very poignant perspectives and opinions from which the whole group could benefit. Below are a few suggestions on how to best include these people.

- Be observant. Look for people who are avidly taking notes or who make side comments to others around them but who don't speak up in large group discussion. These are likely your backstage participants.

- When opening the floor for discussion, try to direct a specific question to the person. "Martha, how would you respond to the statement . . . ?" If Martha gives a short answer or merely shrugs her shoulders, say, "That's okay, Martha. We'll get your response on another topic." If she does share, be sure to thank her and affirm her for her response.

- When breaking the group into small groups, you might ask Martha to facilitate the group's discussion. Ask her to be a spokesperson for the group and to report to the large group on what her group concluded.

- If you know the person well and you see him taking notes or making a side comment, you might make a comment like, "Jack, I just know you have some thoughts on this subject. Come on, won't you share them with us?" Try to solicit and encourage. And when he does respond, affirm his response. "Thanks, Jack. That was a very thought-provoking observation. Does anyone else have something to add to what Jack just said?"

Those Who Take the Opposite Point of View

You say the sky is blue; they say the sky is gray. There are individuals who enjoy taking the opposite point of view, splitting hairs over the meaning of words and philosophizing over the meaning of statements. Their ability to examine facts from every conceivable angle is truly remarkable, but—as with our limelight friends—their input must be confined to the subject at hand.

If you have someone who gets hung up on semantics, wants to take issue with the material that is being presented, or becomes argumentative, try one or more of the following remedies:

- Ask the person to summarize what he thinks the authors' intent was in writing the material. In other words, guide the participant away from his own pontifications and help him to focus on what the authors wanted to convey. You may have to redirect his attention to the authors' point of view several times, explaining that for the purposes of this class, you are focusing on the material as it is presented by the authors.

- If the problem persists and/or the person becomes negative, you may want to talk to him privately. Take time to listen to his opinion. Find out if the material being presented is offensive to him in some way and, if so, why.

- Affirm her for positive contributions made and insights shared. Know your material well enough to dispel any arguments she may bring up to discredit the material being taught. If she voices an opinion that is contrary to what is being presented, counter with something like, "That's a very interesting point that doesn't quite click with what we're trying to accomplish here. I'd be happy to discuss this with you after class, if you wish, when we can explore it further."

Don't feel as if you have to have all the answers. Sometimes, just listening and even offering to do some research can help a negative person warm up a bit and be willing to look at the material from a fresh perspective.

People Who Never Say Anything

In every crowd there are always those people who never say anything. It's not because they're behind-the-scenes people but because they are shy. This doesn't mean they don't have thoughts or opinions. Instead, for whatever reason, they don't feel secure enough to share their opinions in a large group setting. Here are some things to consider with our quiet friends:

- Not everybody verbally expresses what they believe about a statement or question. Be observant. Watch body language—those physical clues that reveal whether a person is bored, excited, angry, happy, or nervous. Learn to read your audience. This is especially important for people who don't talk during class. By watching for their reaction, you may be able to approach them either before or after class to "check in" and find out on a one-on-one basis how they like the class.

- During small group time, check to see if he feels freer to speak in a smaller group setting. If not, you may want to ask a person in the group to engage him in conversation on a one-on-one basis regarding the material that was presented. You can suggest that the person solicit opinions about the video, the exercises, or any of the large- or small-group discussions. Encourage the person to steer clear of questions that would require simply a yes or no response.

General Tips

- Before class, practice the questions you will ask. It's often helpful to say them aloud in front of a mirror. Knowing your group, will the questions elicit response? Can you anticipate any challenges from participants? If so, how will you handle them?

- Express yourself with warmth, sincerity, and interest. If you are enthusiastic about the material, chances are your class will be, too.

- Reword questions as you deem necessary. The material presented is a guideline for you—use it, augment it, or work with it in a way that maintains the integrity of the session yet addresses both your personality and the personalities of the class participants.

- Differences of opinion are okay. If you sense that a difference of opinion is turning negative, you may want to intervene by expressing that for the purposes of these sessions, you're going to stick with what the authors have written.

- People need time to think about statements before they respond. If there is some initial silence, that is okay. Be patient. If the class doesn't begin to respond after fifteen to twenty seconds, try rephrasing the question or statements.
- Be a good listener. Affirm your class and respect their opinions.

A FINAL WORD

Enjoy facilitating this course. How you utilize this resource is limited only by your imagination. Of course, you can lengthen or shorten the sessions to fit your own needs. This course lends itself to a variety of settings, such as Sunday school classes, small group studies, home Bible studies, weekend retreats, seminars or one-day events, and one-on-one coaching. Now relax and enjoy helping other couples learn new skills that will enrich their relationship for a lifetime.

The Second Half of Marriage

LEADER'S GUIDE

Session 1: Getting Ready for the Second Half

---— ✳ ——

LEADER PREPARATION

"Help! I'm Having a Midlife Marriage"

After dropping off their youngest son at college, the Arps weren't sure about the challenges that awaited them as they faced an empty nest at home. That fall they took an "empty nest trip" to New England. After a few days of relaxation, they decided to talk openly about their marriage and to set a course for where they wanted their marriage to go in the future.

They began the process of evaluation by listing some of their best marriage attributes. They looked at their roles as parents, their careers, the way they communicate, their commitment to each other and to God. Then they took an equally careful look at the aspects of their marriage that were not so positive—their stumbling blocks—like overscheduling themselves or assuming that because they worked in marriage education, their marriage was just fine.

Having assessed the positive and not-so-positive parts of their marriage, they began to set goals and plan for the future. Their desire was to "finish well." They realized that marriage is a journey, not a destination, and one that is not without risks. Some of the risks include making yourself vulnerable, self-disclosing in a deeper way, and choosing to grow and adapt to each other through all the stages of marriage and life.

Surveying the Second Half of Marriage

The Arps came back from their empty nest trip ready to search out resources to help them transition into the second half of their marriage. Finding few practical resources and being determined to persevere, the Arps began their own research, having in mind the goal of developing resources that would help other couples who were facing the empty nest years.

They found that "the transition into the second half of marriage is a crisis time for many couples. The current trend is alarming: long-term marriages are breaking up in record numbers."

Both being marriage educators, the Arps "decided to take the initiative. How could we help meet the challenges facing midlife marriages?" To help get a realistic picture of long-term marriages, Dave and Claudia developed a formal written survey that they

---— ✳ ——

Planning Notes

_____

_____

_____

_____

_____

_____

_____

_____

_____

_____

_____

_____

_____

_____

_____

_____

_____

_____

_____

_____

_____

_____

_____

_____

_____

_____

_____

_____

_____

_____

_____

_____

_____

_____

_____

_____

_____

mailed to five thousand people. More than 10 percent responded, giving the Arps a good indication of the marriage climate throughout the United States. These survey results are shared throughout the book and especially throughout the chapter. (Since their initial survey and with the help of marital researchers at the University of Denver, Dave and Claudia have completed another survey, based on their original one, that confirms their initial findings.)

From these results, eight challenges for the second half of marriage were identified:

1. Letting go of past marital disappointments
2. Creating a partner-focused rather than child-focused marriage
3. Maintaining an effective communication system
4. Using anger and conflict creatively to build the relationship
5. Building a deeper, more enjoyable friendship
6. Renewing romance
7. Adjusting to changing roles with aging parents and adult children
8. Evaluating the spiritual side of marriage—relationships to each other and God

WELCOME (5 minutes)

Call the group together and welcome them to the first session of *The Second Half of Marriage*.

Introduce yourself, briefly explaining who you are, a little about your family, your marriage, and so forth, and tell them why you are excited about this course.

Tell them that today's session will cover part 1 in the book, which includes the chapters titled "Help! I'm Having a Midlife Marriage" and "Surveying the Second Half of Marriage." If group members have not already done so, encourage them to read these chapters for themselves, on their own.

Make sure all the participants have a copy of *The Second Half of Marriage Participant's Guide*, which contains the text from the Arps' book *The Second Half of Marriage*.

OPEN IN PRAYER (1 minute)

Father, as we embark on the journey into the second half of our marriages, whether we are already well into the journey or just beginning down the road, we ask that you guide our thoughts, keep us focused, and open our hearts so that our marriages will glorify you. Amen.

Planning Notes

_____

_____

_____

_____

_____

_____

_____

_____

_____

_____

_____

_____

_____

_____

_____

_____

_____

_____

_____

_____

_____

_____

_____

_____

_____

_____

_____

_____

_____

_____

_____

_____

_____

_____

_____

_____

_____

SESSION OVERVIEW (1 minute)

Please turn to page 233. There is some room provided for you to write brief notes to help you remember what we have discussed.

In today's session we'll be covering:

- Symptoms of the second half of marriage
- What other couples report as being important to them in marriage
- Taking your own survey

VIDEO (9 minutes)

On page 234 is space for you to jot down some notes as you watch the introductory video clip with Dave and Claudia Arp. They will explain how they entered into their second half of marriage and how the national survey they conducted became the foundation for this study.

> Show the introductory video clip, which follows the short preview for this course.

MARRIAGE FORUM (8 minutes)

Now turn to page 235. Use the space provided to take notes, if you wish. Dave and Claudia listed some symptoms of the second half of marriage. Before we identify some of those, let's hear from some of you as to why you wanted to take this class. What are some of your expectations?

> Allow a few minutes for people to share their reasons.

Think about where you are at in your marriage. How many believe you are still in the first half of marriage? How many believe you are just entering the second half? And finally, how many of you are already somewhere on the path inside the second half? Anyone believe you are somewhere other than those three places?

How many of you still have children at home? How many have children who left the nest but have moved back home? How many have married children? Grandchildren?

ONE ON ONE (10 minutes)

Please turn to page 236. There you will find written instructions as to what we're going to do next.

Session 1

❧

GETTING READY FOR THE SECOND HALF

OVERVIEW OF THIS SESSION

During today's session we will be discussing:

- Symptoms of the second half of marriage
- What other couples report as being important to them in marriage
- Taking your own survey

VIDEO CLIP NOTES

MARRIAGE FORUM

Why are you taking this class? What do you hope to gain as a result? Are you approaching the beginning of the second half of your marriage, or are you in the middle of it? Is your nest in the process of emptying, or has it just refilled? Perhaps you're in a new marriage but you're in midlife or beyond.

ONE ON ONE

Look at the survey results on pages 34–35. Find your age group for each of the charts given, and share your reactions to each one.

Each couple needs to break away from the group a little and find a place where you can talk quietly. We'll have about 10 minutes to discuss the results of the Arps' survey of long-term marriages, which is on pages 34–35. I want you to look at the charts, find your age group, and share your reactions to each one.

> After 9 minutes have elapsed, give your group a 1-minute warning before moving on to the next segment.

MY REFLECTION TIME (7 minutes)

You can stay where you are, but I want each of you to look at the Marriage Builder on page 47. This is a copy of the survey on which the Arps based their research. Take about 5–7 minutes to complete this survey for yourself. As the Arps pointed out, periodically taking this survey is a good idea. Therefore another copy of this survey is on page 217. The Arps have given permission for you to make several copies of this survey for future use. But for now, let's focus on the one on page 47.

> After 6 minutes have elapsed, give the group a 1-minute warning before continuing on to the next segment.

ONE ON ONE (15 minutes)

Turn to page 237. For this next step, we will go over our survey responses with our spouse. Remember, it is quite possible that your spouse may view things differently than you do. Our goal is not to make the other person conform to our way of thinking but to learn from each other and grow.

As you go over your individual surveys, please discuss the following:

- Areas where your responses are within one point of each other—areas you mutually agree are relatively good, neutral, or need attention.
- Areas where you mildly disagree—a 2- to 3-point difference. Find out why your spouse rated the category the way he or she did. If it is an area you believe needs further discussion, place a check mark next to it and come back to it later when you have more time and privacy to talk.
- Areas where there is a drastic difference of opinion. Definitely flag those areas for discussion at a more opportune time. You will want to wait to discuss emotionally charged issues until we learn some new communication skills in challenges 3 and 4.

---

34 ❧ The Second Half of Marriage

different categories is not as significant as your willingness to discuss them with your spouse and to talk about where you want to be in the future. (After completing this book, you may want to retake the survey and check progress made. Extra surveys are in the appendix on page 217.) Also, if you identified areas for improvement, as you go through this book you will have the opportunity to work on many of them.

Now compare your ratings with the other participants'.

GENERAL SURVEY RESULTS

As we compiled and tabulated responses, we began to see that successful second-half marriages have several commonalities. We were encouraged as we realized that marital satisfaction tends to rise after the children grow up and leave home. However, the lowest time of martial satisfaction, as indicated by our survey, is when adolescent children are present. Consider the following chart:

Response to Questionnaire Answers out of 10	1= very unsatisfied	10= very satisfied		
Aspects of Marriage	**Under 40**	**40–49**	**50–59**	**Over 60**
Financial	5.96	6.58	7.24	8.54
Companionship	7.82	7.54	8.00	9.25
Spiritual Growth	6.36	6.94	7.77	8.65
Mutual Activities	6.43	6.70	7.24	8.49
Individual Activities	7.01	7.29	7.75	8.33
Communication	6.57	6.68	7.16	7.69
My Health	5.77	6.39	6.71	7.65
Mate's Health	6.11	6.91	6.85	7.71
Ministry	6.68	6.82	7.05	7.48
Friends & Family	7.07	7.17	7.51	8.48
Community	6.31	6.12	6.44	7.39
Romance	6.33	6.60	6.95	8.20
Household Resp.	6.58	6.97	7.78	8.32
Conflict Resolution	6.42	6.32	6.88	8.29
Sex	6.97	7.12	7.24	8.14
Education	6.94	7.16	7.63	8.27
Relationship/Children	7.66	7.31	8.04	8.68
Relationship/Grandchildren	low data	low data	6.18	9.10
Retirement	5.69	5.95	6.58	8.44
Relation/Aging Parents	7.33	6.34	7.14	8.73

Surveying the Second Half of Marriage ❧ 35

BEST, WORST, FEARS, AND DREAMS

Let's look at the four essay questions. For each, we've summarized the answers we received, and then listed some typical comments.

What Are the Best Aspects of Your Marriage?

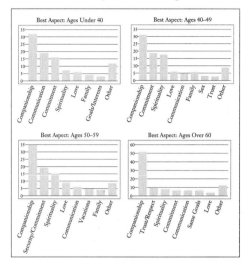

"Our friendship and the ability to work together on common goals."
"Strong communication skills, and we build each other up constantly."
"We are each other's best friend and really enjoy being together."
"My husband is my best friend, my confidant, my lover."
"Spiritual commitment and commitment to each other."

Surveying the Second Half of Marriage ❧ 47

MARRIAGE BUILDER

Surveying the Second Half of Marriage

Check your level of satisfaction in the following general categories as they relate to your marriage:

Areas of satisfaction or dissatisfaction:

	very dissatisfied	neither		very satisfied
	1 2 3	4 5 6	7 8	9 10
Financial management				
Companionship				
Spiritual growth and commitment				
Mutual activities				
Individual activities				
Communication with mate				
My health and physical fitness				
Mate's health and physical fitness				
Ministry activities				
Friends and extended family				
Community service				
Romance and intimacy				
Household responsibilities				
Conflict resolution				
Sexual fulfillment				
Education and career development				
Relationship with children				
Relationship with grandchildren				
Retirement plan				
Relationship with aging parents				

1. What are the best aspects of your marriage?

2. What are the areas that cause the greatest stress in your marriage?

3. What do you fear the most about your marriage in the future?

4. What are you looking forward to in your marriage in the future?

Surveying Your Marriage

❧

Surveying the Second Half of Marriage

Check your level of satisfaction in the following general categories as they relate to your marriage:

Areas of satisfaction or dissatisfaction:

	very dissatisfied	neither		very satisfied
	1 2 3	4 5 6	7 8	9 10
Financial management				
Companionship				
Spiritual growth and commitment				
Mutual activities				
Individual activities				
Communication with mate				
My health and physical fitness				
Mate's health and physical fitness				
Ministry activities				
Friends and extended family				
Community service				
Romance and intimacy				
Household responsibilities				
Conflict resolution				
Sexual fulfillment				
Education and career development				
Relationship with children				
Relationship with grandchildren				
Retirement plan				
Relationship with aging parents				

1. What are the best aspects of your marriage?

2. What are the areas that cause the greatest stress in your marriage?

3. What do you fear the most about your marriage in the future?

4. What are you looking forward to in your marriage in the future?

Permission granted to copy this page for personal use only.

Session 1: Getting Ready for the Second Half ❧ 237

MY REFLECTION TIME

Take a moment to complete the Marriage Builder ("Surveying the Second Half of Marriage") on page 47. There is another survey form on page 217 for you to copy and use at later dates, as you desire.

ONE ON ONE

Share your survey with your spouse. Remember, your spouse may see things differently than you do.

• Identify those areas where your responses are within one point of each other—areas you mutually agree are relatively good, neutral, or need attention.

• Identify those areas where you mildly disagree—a 2–3 point difference. Find out why your spouse rated that category the way he or she did. If it is an area you believe needs further discussion, place a check mark to the left of the category for future reference.

• Identify those areas where there is a drastic difference of opinion. Definitely flag those areas but save for later discussion. In challenges 2 and 3 we will learn new skills for discussing our differences in a productive, non-attacking way. For now we're simply performing a marriage checkup and looking at our relationship as it is presently.

• Go over your responses to questions 1–4 that follow the survey. Again, remember that your spouse may very well see things from a different perspective. The objective is not to change your spouse's opinion to match yours. It is rather to help each of you understand the other's viewpoint.

- Your responses to questions 1–4 following the survey. Again, remember that your spouse may see things differently than you do. Keep in mind that the purpose of this survey is to understand your mate's perspective and to evaluate where you are in your marriage right now.

> After 14 minutes have elapsed, give the group a 1-minute warning before proceeding to the wrap-up.

WRAP-UP (5 minutes)

I hope this first session has instilled some excitement as to what the second half of your marriage can be like. As the Arps said in their video clip, "You can make the rest the best!"

Please turn to page 238. Take time this week to complete this Marriage Builder together. You may want to pray as a couple first, asking God to direct your heart, your words, and your marriage.

Find a relaxed place where you can talk freely with your spouse. If you decide to stay at home, turn off the telephone ringer, let the answering machine get your calls, and focus on each other. Record your thoughts—in the space provided, if you wish.

Next go over those areas of the survey you flagged today and identify areas that need some work. Don't try to resolve differences at this point. You're simply agreeing that they exist.

Before we meet again next time, please read the chapter titled "Challenge One: Let Go of Past Marital Disappointments, Forgive Each Other, and Commit to Making the Rest of Your Marriage the Best," which begins on page 51.

Close in Prayer

Father God, we thank you for the gift of marriage you have given us. Thank you that we have made it this far. Give us the strength, commitment, and courage to traverse this new stage of marriage. We ask for your blessing on our marriage and on the work we will be doing together to strengthen it. Help us to truly make the rest the best. Amen.

Planning Notes

_____

_____

_____

_____

_____

_____

_____

_____

_____

_____

_____

_____

_____

_____

_____

_____

MY REFLECTION TIME

Take a moment to complete the Marriage Builder ("Surveying the Second Half of Marriage") on page 47. There is another survey form on page 217 for you to copy and use at later dates, as you desire.

ONE ON ONE

Share your survey with your spouse. Remember, your spouse may see things differently than you do.

- Identify those areas where your responses are within one point of each other—areas you mutually agree are relatively good, neutral, or need attention.

- Identify those areas where you mildly disagree—a 2–3 point difference. Find out why your spouse rated that category the way he or she did. If it is an area you believe needs further discussion, place a check mark to the left of the category for future reference.

- Identify those areas where there is a drastic difference of opinion. Definitely flag those areas but save for later discussion. In challenges 2 and 3 we will learn new skills for discussing our differences in a productive, non-attacking way. For now we're simply performing a marriage checkup and looking at our relationship as it is presently.

- Go over your responses to questions 1–4 that follow the survey. Again, remember that your spouse may very well see things from a different perspective. The objective is not to change your spouse's opinion to match yours. It is rather to help each of you understand the other's viewpoint.

WRAP-UP

Assignments for next session:

1. Complete the Marriage Builder on page 46 and discuss with your spouse.
2. Discuss the survey we completed today and list areas that need some work. Remember to save any emotionally charged issues for after we look at challenges 2 and 3.
3. Read the chapter titled "Challenge One," which begins on page 51.

Challenge One

❧

Let Go of Past Marital Disappointments, Forgive Each Other, and Commit to Making the Rest of Your Marriage the Best

Session 2: Challenge One

———— ✷ ————

LET GO OF PAST MARITAL DISAPPOINTMENTS, FORGIVE EACH OTHER, AND COMMIT TO MAKING THE REST OF YOUR MARRIAGE THE BEST

LEADER PREPARATION

After returning home from their empty nest trip to New England, the Arps decided to make a list of things they would never do again. They say, "For us it was an important step in letting go of unrealistic dreams and expectations and in getting on with our future. We had to admit to each other that some things just were not going to happen. We will never have a daughter; our backs will never be completely healthy again; we'll never ride across the Swiss Alps on a motorcycle; Dave will never grow more hair."

As the years pass, Dave and Claudia's "we'll never do" list continues to grow. They write, "Some things will not change, and that includes some of our little irritations. . . . Dave will always sneak ice cream late at night; Claudia's desk will never be completely decluttered.

"When the children grow up and leave home, these little irritations often become more glaring and, when not dealt with, lead to discouragement and disappointment again and again. . . . When a long-term marriage crumbles, most of the time it isn't because of a major crisis or a one-time event. More likely it's the result of little issues that have built up over the years until they threaten the very foundation of the marriage."

Eventually, if left unresolved, irritations can lead to increased emotional distance. To remedy this, the Arps write, "Before you can regroup and reignite your relationship, you must deal with your own disappointments, let go of past hurts and lost dreams."

Only through this letting-go process can couples come to a real acceptance of each other and a realization that neither of them is perfect. Beyond this realization

———— ✷ ————

Planning Notes

comes forgiveness, which is foundational to a healthy long-term marriage. As Claudia says in the video, "Forgiveness is the oil that lubricates a love relationship, and it's an oil we need daily."

Forgiving little irritations is one thing, but when there are long-standing problems, couples need to realize that it all takes time. "You can't solve in one day what took years to create. However, there are steps that can be taken."

Recognizing that forgiveness is a process, the Arps outline five steps to take toward this goal.

1. *Identify grievances.* Actually make a list. This list is personal—not necessarily to be shared with your spouse.
2. *Evaluate the grievances you listed.* Which ones can be easily forgiven? Which need to be discussed? And which will require a more serious effort, perhaps even professional help? (In the case of abusive situations, seek safety and help immediately, but most grievances will be things you can deal with as a couple.)
3. *Decide to forgive.* Are you willing to forgive your spouse for the items you listed? "Remember, forgiveness begins with a simple decision, a simple act of the will. . . . It is not dependent upon our spouse asking for our forgiveness or even acknowledging he or she has done anything wrong."
4. *Let go.* Ceremoniously let go of the little grievances you listed. Perhaps you will want to burn them or bury them. "Or if appropriate, consider wrapping the list in a box and giving it to your mate with a note saying, 'I promise to never be bothered by these, your previously incredibly irritating but now lovable idiosyncratic behaviors. This is my gift to you for the second half of our marriage.'" For issues that need more work, discuss them with your mate. Seek out professional counseling, if necessary.
5. *Change your responses now that you've forgiven your spouse.* "The next time you sense irritation rising, try to turn the situation around by replacing your negative response with loving encouragement for your spouse."

One more list that is important to make is a list of "things we will do in the second half of marriage." This will help you to make the rest of your marriage the best. The Arps' list included:

- We will release and let go of our missed dreams and disappointments with each other, with our children, with our parents, and with ourselves.
- We will accept each other as a package deal.
- We will forgive and ask for forgiveness when needed.
- We will renew our commitment to each other and to growing together in the second half of our marriage.

Planning Notes

_____
_____
_____
_____
_____
_____
_____
_____
_____
_____
_____
_____
_____
_____
_____
_____
_____
_____
_____
_____
_____
_____
_____
_____
_____
_____
_____
_____
_____
_____
_____
_____
_____
_____
_____
_____
_____
_____

If you are willing to recommit yourself to your spouse and to your marriage, you can handle disappointments and move on in your marriage. You can reconnect and build an even deeper, more personal relationship in the second half. Pointing to their national survey, the Arps write, "For those couples who choose to forgive and to grow together, we are happy to report that marital satisfaction goes up. For those couples, the best *is* yet to be!"

WELCOME (1 minute)

> Call the group together and welcome them to the second session of *The Second Half of Marriage.* Explain that today's session begins focusing on the eight challenges identified by the Arps' national marriage survey. We will start with challenge 1: letting go of past marital disappointments, forgiving each other, and committing to make the rest of your marriage the best.

OPEN IN PRAYER (1 minute)

God, today we're going to begin looking at some of the challenges couples face during the second half of marriage. Today's topic deals with letting go of missed dreams and unrealistic expectations, and being willing to forgive each other. You have asked us to forgive others just as you have forgiven us. Help us to do just that. Then help us to let go of the past and renew our commitment to our partners for the second half of our marriage. Amen.

REVIEW OF SESSION ONE (1 minute)

During our last session, we looked at the symptoms of the second half of marriage to identify those who are entering into or are already in this stage. We also took a look at what other couples reported as being important to them in marriage. And we took our own surveys individually, comparing our responses with those of our spouse.

SESSION TWO OVERVIEW (1 minute)

Please turn to page 239. For this session we will be discussing:

- Releasing unrealistic expectations by making a "we'll never do" list
- Forgiving each other through a five-step process
- Renewing our commitment by making a "things we will do in the second half of marriage" list

Planning Notes

_____

_____

_____

_____

_____

_____

_____

_____

_____

_____

_____

_____

_____

_____

_____

_____

_____

Session 2

———— ❧ ————

CHALLENGE ONE
LET GO OF PAST MARITAL DISAPPOINTMENTS, FORGIVE EACH OTHER, AND COMMIT TO MAKING THE REST OF YOUR MARRIAGE THE BEST

OVERVIEW OF THIS SESSION

During today's session we will discuss:

- Releasing unrealistic expectations by making a "we'll never do" list

- Forgiving each other through a five-step process

- Renewing our commitment by making a "things we will do in the second half of marriage" list

———— ❧ ————

239

_____

_____

_____

_____

_____

_____

_____

_____

_____

_____

_____

_____

_____

_____

_____

_____

VIDEO (16 minutes)

You may find it helpful to jot down some notes during the video clip, in the space provided on page 240. During this segment, Dave and Claudia will speak openly about their own experience of transitioning into the empty nest and how they were able to let go of past disappointments, forgive each other, and commit to making the rest of their marriage the best.

> Show the video clip for challenge 1.

MARRIAGE FORUM (5 minutes)

In the video segment, the Arps talked about making their own "we'll never do" list and how freeing this exercise was for them. What are some of the things couples facing the empty nest years might put on their "we'll never do" list? You can use the space provided on page 241 to jot down some notes as we discuss this.

> Allow some time for people to respond.

ONE ON ONE (5 minutes)

Now let's get more personal. What are some of the things you would put on your own list? Please turn to page 242. Let's break into our one-on-one groups and take some time now to begin making our own "we'll never do" list on page 243.

> After 4 minutes have elapsed, give your group a 1-minute warning before moving on to the next segment.

MARRIAGE FORUM (5 minutes)

Now that you have at least started your list, let's talk about how important forgiveness is in the second half of marriage. Please turn to page 244. Does anybody here have a perfect mate? Does anybody here have a mate who *thinks* he or she is perfect? We all have little irritating habits that will probably never change, but we can accept each other as a package deal. And that involves forgiving each other.

VIDEO CLIP NOTES

MARRIAGE FORUM

What are some of the things couples in the empty nest years will probably never do?

ONE ON ONE

What are those things that you will never do? Or what things just aren't going to happen? Make your own list.

Our "We'll Never Do" List

MARRIAGE FORUM

What are some of the obstacles to forgiving others for things they have said or done? What would make forgiveness easier?

MY REFLECTION TIME

Read the "Decide to Forgive" section starting on page 58. Do you need to go through this five-step process? (You may want to wait until you can find a quiet, private place to complete these steps.)

- What value is there in forming a grievance list?

- When should such a list be discussed with a spouse, and when should it remain private?

- In evaluating the severity of grievances, what criteria do you think should be used to determine whether they are mere irritations or serious?

- How do you feel about the Arps' statement that "forgiveness begins with a simple decision, a simple act of the will"?

- What makes it difficult to let go of past hurts? What would make it easier?

As God's chosen people, holy and dearly loved, clothe yourselves with compassion, kindness, humility, gentleness and patience.

What are some of the obstacles to forgiving others (especially our partners) for things they have said or done? What would make forgiveness easier?

Has anyone had an experience in which you have received forgiveness from someone else? What did that feel like?

Allow some time for people to respond.

MY REFLECTION TIME (5 minutes)

In a few moments we're going to have time to reflect on the steps of forgiveness. Once you are settled, read the "Decide to Forgive" section, which starts on page 58. If you want to begin working through these steps of forgiveness on your own during this session, that's fine. If you would rather do this another time, think about the following questions:

- What value is there in making a grievance list?
- When should such a list be discussed with a spouse, and when should it remain private?
- In evaluating the severity of grievances, what criteria do you think should be used to determine whether they are mere irritations or serious?
- How do you feel about the Arps' statement that "forgiveness begins with a simple decision, a simple act of the will"?
- What makes it difficult to let go of past hurts and missed dreams? What would make it easier?

After 4 minutes have elapsed, give your group a 1-minute warning before moving on to the next segment. To bring this reflection time to a close, read Colossians 3:12–14.

Turn to page 245 and follow along with me as I read Colossians 3:12–14. It's a wonderful description of the attributes of an enriched, growing long-term marriage.

As God's chosen people, holy and dearly loved, clothe yourselves with compassion, kindness, humility, gentleness and patience. Bear with each other and forgive whatever grievances you may have against once another. Forgive as the Lord forgave you. And over all these virtues put on love, which binds them all together in perfect unity.

Planning Notes

_____

_____

_____

_____

_____

_____

_____

_____

_____

_____

_____

_____

_____

_____

_____

---

244 ❧ The Second Half of Marriage Participant's Guide

MARRIAGE FORUM

What are some of the obstacles to forgiving others for things they have said or done? What would make forgiveness easier?

MY REFLECTION TIME

Read the "Decide to Forgive" section starting on page 58. Do you need to go through this five-step process? (You may want to wait until you can find a quiet, private place to complete these steps.)

- What value is there in forming a grievance list?

- When should such a list be discussed with a spouse, and when should it remain private?

- In evaluating the severity of grievances, what criteria do you think should be used to determine whether they are mere irritations or serious?

- How do you feel about the Arps' statement that "forgiveness begins with a simple decision, a simple act of the will"?

- What makes it difficult to let go of past hurts? What would make it easier?

As God's chosen people, holy and dearly loved, clothe yourselves with compassion, kindness, humility, gentleness and patience.

---

58 ❧ The Second Half of Marriage

"I've always tried to grab the best from the past and focus on the future. Because my marriage is so precious to me, I haven't been willing to throw it away because 'I'm right' in a situation and he is wrong. Also, a long time ago I realized it's much easier to put things back together in the framework of a marriage, so I never considered divorce."

Decide to Forgive

Is there something right now that disappoints you about your mate or your relationship? Grievances can range in intensity from habitually leaving the TV on to having illicit affairs. No matter where your disappointments and hurts fall on the continuum, you must decide to forgive your spouse and move beyond these grievances before you can work on developing an exuberant, growing marriage in the second half. Keep in mind that some issues may necessitate the help of a professional counselor or pastor—please seek out this help if you just can't find a way to let go of your anger and pain.

If, however, your issues lie more toward your mate not maintaining the figure you fell in love with or not helping with the dishes after dinner, it's time to let go and move on. Here's the process we suggest to move you toward forgiveness:

Identify grievances. OK, here's the list you may have rattled off in your head, or to your spouse, a thousand times. Now write it down! You won't show this list to your mate (you'll burn it or bury it when you're through), but you need to articulate to yourself once and for all every little thing that continually crops up in your relationship. So do it now!

Evaluate grievances. Now take this list and evaluate which issues can be easily forgiven and forgotten (like leaving tissues in the kitchen sink), which issues need some special closure because they still cause you some pain (your mate's refusal to take up your favorite hobby), which issues need to be discussed because you're still not sure it's time to let them go (people can always loose a few pounds, right?), and which issues will take a serious effort on your part, perhaps even professional intervention, to overcome (affairs, no lovemaking, abusive communication patterns).

Session 2 ❧ 245

Bear with each other and forgive whatever grievances you may have against one another. Forgive as the Lord forgave you. And over all these virtues put on love, which binds them all together in perfect unity.

COLOSSIANS 3:12–14

MARRIAGE FORUM

What are some things couples might like to do in the second half of their marriage?

ONE ON ONE

What are the things you want to do in the second half of your marriage?

MARRIAGE FORUM (5 minutes)

Once we have committed ourselves to working through the steps of forgiveness, it's time to move on and recommit ourselves to our partner and to the second half of our marriage. The Arps talked about making another list of things they were going to do in the second half of their marriage. Let's brainstorm some possible answers typical couples might give. What might go on such a list?

> Allow some time for people to respond.

ONE ON ONE (10 minutes)

Turn to page 63 and read what Dave and Claudia wrote on their "things we will do in the second half of marriage" list. Now it's your turn to make your own list. We're going to break into our one-on-one groups. You will find a place to write your list on page 245.

> After 9 minutes have elapsed, give your group a 1-minute warning before moving on to the next segment.

WRAP-UP (5 minutes)

We've come to the end of the first challenge. We've looked at how to let go of disappointments. We've discussed the importance of forgiveness and of making a fresh commitment to our marriage for the second half. To surmount this challenge will be an ongoing process but one that will make our marriage the best yet.

Please turn to pages 64–65. I encourage each and every one of you to take time this week to complete this Marriage Builder. Do this Marriage Builder independently—especially question 5. Put into practice this week some of the things you listed for questions 1 and 2. If you identified an area where you need to show some patience (question 3), resolve to show more tolerance. Also, complete the list in item 6 and share it with your spouse at a time when you are both relaxed and open. Toward the end of the week, complete question 4. Did your spouse recognize whatever you did as an act of love?

Before we meet for our next session, please read the chapter titled "Challenge Two: Create a Marriage That Is Partner-Focused Rather Than Child-Focused," which begins on page 67.

Bear with each other and forgive whatever grievances you may have against one another. Forgive as the Lord forgave you. And over all these virtues put on love, which binds them all together in perfect unity.

COLOSSIANS 3:12–14

MARRIAGE FORUM

What are some things couples might like to do in the second half of their marriage?

ONE ON ONE

What are the things you want to do in the second half of your marriage?

❧

MARRIAGE BUILDER

The Kindness-Compassion-Patience-Love-Forgiveness Test
(Colossians 3:12–14)

1. Kindness: grace, generosity, friendliness, accommodation.
   How could you express kindness to your mate today, in your words and in your actions?

2. Compassion: tenderness, clemency, sympathy, commiseration.
   When was the last time you showed compassion for your spouse?

3. Patience: forbearance, submission, endurance, constancy, long-sufferingness.
   Has your patience become a little frayed? Is there a situation right now that would benefit from a big dose of patience?

4. Love: affection, charity, friendship, regard, devotion, benevolence, fervor.
   Love is not a nebulous emotion. Love is an attitude of caring more for the other person than for yourself. And love is expressed in little acts of kindness. List ways you have shown love in the past week.

5. Forgiveness: pardon, mercy, acquittal, absolution, reprieve, excuse.
   (We suggest you meditate alone on this part of the Marriage Builder exercise so it will remain a "marriage builder.")
   Are there things for which you need to ask your spouse for forgiveness?

   Is there something you need to forgive your spouse for?

---

6. Make a list:
   You may want to make a list of your mate's positive traits, just as you made a list of his or her shortcomings. Think about what is right about your marriage. What are the positive qualities of your spouse?

Challenge Two

❧

Create a Marriage That Is Partner-Focused
Rather Than Child-Focused

Close in Prayer

Father, we ask that you would go before us this week. Help us to be creative in finding ways to express love, compassion, patience, and kindness to our spouse. As we look over our lists of positive traits, let the time we spend together enrich our marriage and help us to move into a deeper and more loving relationship. Amen.

Planning Notes

_____
_____
_____
_____
_____
_____
_____
_____
_____
_____
_____
_____
_____
_____
_____
_____
_____
_____
_____
_____
_____
_____
_____
_____
_____
_____
_____
_____
_____
_____
_____
_____
_____
_____

Session 3: Challenge Two

———— ✇ ————

CREATE A MARRIAGE THAT IS PARTNER-FOCUSED RATHER THAN CHILD-FOCUSED

LEADER PREPARATION

The Arps write, "During the parenting years, our relationship was focused around the demands of parenting and career rather than around our marriage. Now that our children were grown, we no longer had their activities or crises as a focus."

Dave and Claudia now had time to invest in their relationship, but initially they went from a child-focused relationship to a work-focused relationship. They accepted too many speaking engagements, signed too many book contracts, and were right back on overload. For other couples, feelings of uneasiness creep in as they discover they have more and more time alone together. Many find that with the children gone, their "buffers" are also gone. The quick fixes of the past are not sufficient for the larger blocks of time they now experience.

If empty nest couples are to survive all this additional togetherness, they will need to deepen their friendship and build a relationship that is centered around each other. It's a great time to redefine your marriage and deepen your relationship.

The Arps also had to surmount this challenge. For two highly motivated and equally active people, this was not an easy task. They realized that marriages go through various transitional times. Much like a roller coaster, there are the extreme highs (like those experienced in the earliest stages of marriage) and the dramatic dips (like when the children were going through adolescence).

Statistically, transitional times can be risky times in a relationship. Because people grow and change at different rates and in different ways, when the kids leave home many couples find that they have grown apart. While a marriage may be functional, the Arps write that "a relationship without emotional intimacy is certainly not exciting and is all too often terminal. Yet the good news is that for couples who survive the empty nest and choose to refocus their marriage on their partner, marital satisfaction again rises. But be prepared for changes!"

———— ✇ ————

Planning Notes

As we grow older, roles often change. Women tend to shift from being nurturing to being more interested in tasks and accomplishments, just as men shift from being work-oriented to being more expressive and emotionally responsive. Women often go back to school or pick up their career once again, while men tend to focus more on home and relationships.

During the transition into the empty nest years, couples need to focus on rebuilding intimacy and companionship. For years, by necessity, they have focused on parenting. Now is the time to refocus on each other. They need to make the most of private moments. By nurturing their friendship, they can build a relationship that is even more fulfilling and meaningful.

For the Arps, a companionship marriage means a partner-focused marriage—one in which the goals are for the betterment of the couple, not just an individual. Conversely, a marriage that is not partner-focused is individual-focused. Claudia writes, "When both spouses want their own way, they don't have a companionship or partner-focused marriage. Sometimes one spouse is active, the other spouse passive. Or there's little passion, intimacy, or sense of we-ness."

Often these marriages are held together by sheer determination. Dave writes, "The marriage is being held together by [the couple's] commitment to never give up no matter how bad it gets. Those who responded to our survey and said that the best thing about their marriage was their children or anything other than their spouse would be in this category."

In order to have a nurturing marriage, couples must be willing to be fluid—"adjusting to each other and striving to be partner focused. The survival of a long-term marriage depends on the complex process of mutual adjustment of the two people to each other."

Claudia mentioned "we-ness"—ways in which a couple can grow together. Perhaps they can shop together or do chores together. Many couples take up golfing or walking together. But developing this we-ness and a companionship marriage is not without some cautions.

"In a companionship marriage, couples have greater expectations for their marriage relationship," the Arps write. "Their quest for intimacy leads to a degree of closeness that at the same time can generate conflict."

However, with perseverance and commitment, a marriage in the second half can be rewarding. The Arps' mentors, Drs. David and Vera Mace, indicate there are "three essentials for a growing marriage:

1. A commitment to growth
2. An effectively functioning communication system
3. The ability to make creative use of conflict."

Planning Notes

_____

_____

_____

_____

_____

_____

_____

_____

_____

_____

_____

_____

_____

_____

_____

_____

_____

_____

_____

_____

_____

_____

_____

_____

_____

_____

_____

_____

_____

_____

_____

_____

_____

_____

WELCOME (1 minute)

Call the group together and welcome them to the third session of *The Second Half of Marriage.* Explain that today's session will focus on challenge 2: creating a partner-focused rather than a child-focused marriage.

OPEN IN PRAYER (1 minute)

Thank you, God, that in your divine plan, you created marriage to be a long-term commitment. As we move into the empty nest stage of life, help us to refocus our attention and interests on our spouse. Help us to find renewed joy and excitement as we develop a companionship marriage that focuses on us as a couple instead of as individuals. Open our minds and hearts today as we face this challenge together. Amen.

REVIEW SESSION TWO (1 minute)

During session 2 we talked about letting go of unrealistic expectations, being willing to accept and forgive each other, and recommitting ourselves to our marriage in the second half. We also discussed the five-step process toward forgiveness: identify grievances, evaluate grievances, decide to forgive, let go, and change your responses. Finally, we developed our lists of "things we will do in the second half of marriage."

SESSION THREE OVERVIEW (1 minute)

Please turn to page 247. During this session we will discuss:

- How roles change as men and women reach the empty nest years
- How to move from a child-focused to a partner-focused relationship
- Creatively promoting "we-ness" in our marriage relationships

VIDEO (10 minutes)

On page 248 space is provided for you to make notes as you listen to Dave and Claudia talk about building a partner-focused marriage. They will share a little about how men and women tend to change when the kids grow up and are no longer the focus, and how these changes can help couples develop a closer, more personal relationship.

Planning Notes

_____

_____

_____

_____

_____

_____

_____

_____

_____

_____

_____

_____

_____

_____

_____

_____

_____

_____

_____

_____

_____

_____

_____

_____

_____

_____

_____

_____

_____

_____

_____

_____

_____

_____

Session 3

❧

CHALLENGE TWO
CREATE A MARRIAGE THAT IS PARTNER-FOCUSED RATHER THAN CHILD-FOCUSED

OVERVIEW OF THIS SESSION

During this session we will discuss:

- How roles change as men and women reach the empty nest years

- How to move from a child-focused to a partner-focused relationship

- Creatively promoting "we-ness" in our marriage relationships

❧

247

VIDEO CLIP NOTES

> Show the video clip for challenge 2.

MARRIAGE FORUM (10 minutes)

Refer to your topics on page 249. There is room for you to take notes as we share our ideas together.

What are some of the roller-coaster highs and lows most marriages experience?

> Give couples a few minutes to respond.

What do you believe are common obstacles many couples face as they enter their second half of marriage?

> Give couples a few minutes to respond.

What are some of the dynamic changes that relationships experience in the empty nest? How do roles change when children grow up?

> Give couples a few minutes to respond.

What is your idea of intimacy and companionship? And what obstacles do you believe couples might face in achieving goals related to them?

> Give couples a few minutes to respond.

ONE ON ONE (10 minutes)

In a couple of minutes we're going to break into our one-on-one groups. But for now please look at pages 249–250. There you will see the topics you are to discuss as couples. We'll take 10 minutes to discuss these and then get back together as a large group to share ideas.

> Give couples a minute to get situated and start talking. After 9 minutes give the group a 1-minute warning. Conclude this one-on-one time after 10 minutes. Couples can remain where they are seated for the next segment.

Planning Notes

_____

_____

_____

_____

_____

_____

_____

_____

_____

_____

_____

_____

_____

_____

_____

_____

_____

_____

_____

_____

_____

_____

_____

_____

_____

_____

_____

_____

_____

_____

_____

_____

Session 3 ❧ 249

MARRIAGE FORUM

1. Roller-coaster highs and lows, and how long they lasted
2. Common obstacles when entering the second half of marriage
3. Dynamic changes couples face in this time of transition—how roles and focus change
4. Definitions of intimacy and companionship

ONE ON ONE

Please discuss the following questions and be prepared to share some of your ideas with the rest of the group.

1. Identify some of the roller-coaster highs in your marriage, as well as some of the low points. Over the years, what crises have you weathered?

2. How have your roles changed, or what changes do you anticipate in the second half?

---

250 ❧ The Second Half of Marriage Participant's Guide

3. Define intimacy and companionship as you would like to see them applied to your own marriage. As you think about achieving greater intimacy and companionship and becoming more partner-focused, what are some of the obstacles you face?

4. Come up with at least five ways in which you can develop more we-ness in your marriage—perhaps things you formerly did as individuals that you could do together, or activities neither of you have done before that you would like to explore together.

MARRIAGE FORUM

Ideas shared by others regarding:

1. Developing a more partner-focused marriage

MARRIAGE FORUM

Now let's talk about how we can refocus on our partners. The Arps talked about how a second-half marriage is held together from within. Use the space provided on pages 250 and 251 to jot down notes, if you wish. What are some practical things we could do to develop a more partner-focused marriage?

> Give couples a few minutes to respond.

What are some of the ideas you came up with to develop we-ness in your relationship?

> Give couples a few minutes to respond.

MY REFLECTION TIME (5 minutes)

Please turn to page 80. There is a section there called "Meet Esther and Ralph." Please read that section individually. See if you identify with this couple. When you are finished, think about the following:

- What changes can you anticipate as you delve into the empty nest years?
- What will it mean in terms of the time you will spend with one another?
- What obstacles will you need to overcome, and what ideas can you generate now that will help you meet these challenges?
- What is the one thing that scares each of you the most about the empty nest and the second half of life?
- What is the one thing that excites you most as you anticipate this stage of life?

> After 4 minutes have elapsed, give your group a 1-minute warning before moving on to the next segment.

ONE ON ONE (15 minutes)

Spend the rest of the time talking with your partner about the above list.

Planning Notes

_____

_____

_____

_____

_____

_____

_____

_____

_____

_____

_____

_____

_____

_____

_____

_____

_____

_____

---

3. Define intimacy and companionship as you would like to see them applied to your own marriage. As you think about achieving greater intimacy and companionship and becoming more partner-focused, what are some of the obstacles you face?

4. Come up with at least five ways in which you can develop more we-ness in your marriage—perhaps things you formerly did as individuals that you could do together, or activities neither of you have done before that you would like to explore together.

MARRIAGE FORUM

Ideas shared by others regarding:

1. Developing a more partner-focused marriage

---

2. We-ness ideas

MY REFLECTION TIME

Read the section called "Meet Esther and Ralph," starting on page 80. Then think about the following:

1. What changes can we anticipate as we delve into the empty nest years?
2. What will it mean in terms of the time we will spend with one another?
3. What obstacles will we need to overcome, and what ideas can we generate now that will help us meet these challenges?
4. What is the one thing that scares me the most about the empty nest and the second half of life?
5. What is the one thing that excites me most as I anticipate this stage of life?

ONE ON ONE

With your partner discuss Esther and Ralph and the above five questions.

---

life. In challenge 3 we'll look at how you can hone your communication skills.

The third essential part of our coping system is our commitment to work through our disagreements and each angry situation that arises. From the Maces we learned that both love *and* anger are positive forces in building a healthy marriage. They give balance and keep us from becoming enmeshed. Every marriage has conflict. Yet too often, in the middle of conflict, anger explodes and destroys, rather than builds, the marriage relationship. So we must learn to positively process anger and release its energy to grow our relationship. In challenge 4 we'll talk more about how to process anger in the second half of marriage.

Transition times in marriage provide us with opportunities to test our coping system! Adjustments are often needed, especially at the beginning of the second half of marriage.

MEET ESTHER AND RALPH

At a neighborhood party, we met Esther and Ralph, who were a living example of a couple who had successfully met the challenge to refocus on each other. Their coping system was functioning, and they had a spark in their relationship that had not always been there. Here is their story:

"When our kids left home, we didn't know each other," Ralph commented.

"It was frightening," Esther added. "We were strangers. For years the children had been our focus. We were good parents. We set goals for our children but never considered setting goals for our marriage. Our lives revolved around our kids and their activities. We had few conflicts; we got along. We loved each other, but when the kids left home, there was a vacuum. We realized we didn't know each other. It was a crisis time in our marriage."

"Plus, the rules changed," Ralph continued. "Esther changed. In the past, Esther was passive; she went along with what I wanted. But when the kids left home, she began to speak up—to be more assertive. I didn't know what was happening!"

After 14 minutes have elapsed, give your group a 1-minute warning before moving into the last segment.

WRAP-UP (5 minutes)

Please turn to page 252. I hope that you are beginning to creatively face some of the challenges that we're discussing in our time together. It will be exciting to see how each of us develops a deeper friendship and intimacy with our spouse as time goes on.

To help you continue on your way, please turn to page 83. The Arps suggest you find a comfortable place to go and talk about the questions in this Marriage Builder. These questions are designed to help you refocus on each other.

Also, before we meet next time, please read the chapter titled "Challenge Three: Maintain an Effective Communication System That Allows You to Express Your Deepest Feelings, Joys, and Concerns," which begins on page 85.

Close in Prayer

Dear heavenly Father, your Word says that you will guide us and counsel us with your eye upon us. How comforting to know that you will be our constant companion as we go through the changes in our marriages and in our lives. Help us to focus on the life partner you have given us. Help us to find ways to develop we-ness in our relationship. Amen.

Planning Notes

_____

_____

_____

_____

_____

_____

_____

_____

_____

_____

_____

_____

_____

_____

_____

_____

_____

---

252 ❧ The Second Half of Marriage Participant's Guide

WRAP-UP

Assignments for next session:

1. Complete the Marriage Builder on page 83.
2. Read the chapter titled "Challenge Three," which begins on page 85.

Challenge Two ❧ 83

❧

MARRIAGE BUILDER

*Question for Reflection: Creating a More
Partner-Focused Marriage*

Following are some reflective questions to think about and mull over. Why not invite your mate to go with you to your favorite coffee shop, and over two cups of coffee or cappuccino, you can talk about the following things. Go on and take the challenge. Your marriage is worth it!

1. On a scale of one to ten (ten being the most), how much we-ness do you have in your marriage relationship?

2. How would you describe your marriage style?

3. What opportunities have you taken to grow your marriage?
   —In the first half of your marriage?

   —In the last twelve months?

4. Have you redefined your roles for the second half?

5. What are some things you can do to develop a more partner-focused marriage?

6. What opportunities for growth are you facing in your marriage at the present time?

7. Would you be willing to read one book dealing with an area of your marriage in which you would like to grow?

Challenge Three

❧

*Maintain an Effective Communication
System That Allows You to Express Your Deepest
Feelings, Joys, and Concerns*

85

Session 4: Challenge Three

Maintain an Effective Communication System That Allows You to Express Your Deepest Feelings, Joys, and Concerns

Leader Preparation

Why does communication in marriage resemble dirty laundry? Dave and Claudia say, "It's easy to get so involved with life challenges that we let our communication slide. Issues we need to discuss pile up like our dirty clothes, and then when we're most stressed out (like late at night), we trip over them. Too tired to deal with them, we stuff them in our marriage storage shed, where they sour and mildew."

Dr. John Gottman, professor of psychology at the University of Washington in Seattle, maintains that for every negative interaction between a couple, there needs to be five positive ones. When we fail to make that ratio and accentuate the negative, the person being criticized goes into "system overload" or "feeling flooded."

To develop more effective and less threatening communication, Dave and Claudia recommend a two-step approach.

1. Evaluate your present communication system.
2. Share your feelings with one another, learning to communicate on a more personal level.

Couples find that the communication patterns they used during the first half of their marriage are often inadequate for the second half. The old ways just don't work anymore. But before changes can be made, couples need to identify their pattern of communication. Dave and Claudia have identified three negative patterns to avoid and one positive pattern that we need to develop. Consider the three negative patterns that typical couples use: avoider-confronter, conflict-avoiding, and conflict-confronting. Then consider the fourth, positive pattern.

Planning Notes

1. The Avoider-Confronter Couple

The avoider often retreats into his or her own world. He prefers to ignore problems and let them slide. For the most part, avoiders are uncomfortable talking about their feelings. Often the husband is the avoider in the relationship and makes the classic stonewalling response. He simply withdraws. The confronter, on the other hand, has no trouble expressing his or her feelings. Often the wife is the confronter. She may enjoy intense conversation and isn't afraid to speak up but easily gets entangled in negative, unproductive confrontations.

2. The Conflict-Avoiding Couple

Conflict-avoiding couples may work well together in many areas, such as building their careers, parenting their children, or volunteering to work at church. However, they lack a close personal relationship. When it comes to deep, intimate conversation or dealing with personal issues, they are distant from one another. One spouse may avoid issues by overadapting, while the other spouse avoids conflict by spending more time at work. Neither is good at handling negative feelings. Instead of expressing and dealing with negative feelings, they stuff them inside. A real danger in this type of marriage, in which there is little intimacy or closeness, is the temptation of extramarital affairs.

3. The Conflict-Confronting Couple

The conflict-confronting couple has no lack of communication; however, much of it is negative and hurtful. Instead of dealing with conflict, they vent their frustrations—to the point that effective communication is stifled. The Arps write, "Confrontations lead to counterconfrontations, and soon you may find yourself in a shouting match and saying things you later regret."

4. The Interpersonally Competent Couple

Much better is to become an interpersonally competent couple.

This involves working on developing new and better ways to communicate and learning to use conflict constructively. These skills will help you build a close and personal relationship with each other and will help you learn to appreciate the other person's attributes and to focus on the positive.

According to the Arps, "No stage of marriage has greater potential for developing interpersonal competence than the second half of marriage. And you have already taken the first step in becoming an interpersonally competent person, if you have committed yourself to having a growing companionship marriage."

Planning Notes

To develop a more intimate marriage, a couple needs to develop what family sociologist Nelson Foote calls "interpersonal competence." And the first step is for the couple to learn how to communicate their innermost feelings, thoughts, and wishes in the context of a supportive relationship. You can learn when to be silent and when to speak up in a nonconfronting way. Dave and Claudia offer seven tips for talking on a more personal level.

1. *Learn to listen.* According to James 1:19, we are to be "quick to listen, slow to speak and slow to become angry."

2. *Be aware of the nonverbal message.* In a study Kodak did on interpersonal communication, they learned that over half of the message (55 percent) is nonverbal. Tone of voice accounts for 38 percent, while the actual words comprised only 7 percent.

3. *Learn to communicate your feelings.* 1 Thessalonians 5:11 tells us to "encourage one another and build each other up." Often we're good at expressing our negative feelings but hesitant to express tender or positive thoughts. We do need to share negative feelings too, but in such a way that attacks the problem, not the person.

4. *Use "I" statements; avoid "you" statements and "why" questions.* "You" statements and "why" questions tend to be viewed as attacking. Let your statements reflect back on you, by using" I" statements.

5. *Learn to complete the communication cycle.* Mirror back to your spouse what he or she just said, to make sure you completely understood the message. "This is what I heard you say . . ." can help keep the communication cycle going.

6. *Agree not to attack the other person or to defend yourself.* If there is a misunderstanding, go back to tip number 5 and complete the communication cycle rather than going on the attack or the defensive.

7. *Have regular couple-communication times.* Daily, if possible, touch base with each other and share what's going on. Often you can touch base while doing a simple task together, like cleaning up the kitchen after breakfast.

Sorry, no shortcuts allowed. Dave and Claudia write, "Remember: deep, intimate, personal conversations don't just happen. You make them happen through lots of hard work. It will take time and effort, but you can restore your passion for your marriage. You can have intimate conversations for two!"

Planning Notes

_____

_____

_____

_____

_____

_____

_____

_____

_____

_____

_____

_____

_____

_____

_____

_____

_____

_____

_____

_____

_____

_____

_____

_____

_____

_____

_____

_____

_____

_____

_____

_____

_____

WELCOME (1 minute)

Call the group together and welcome them to the fourth session of *The Second Half of Marriage.* Tell them that this session will focus on the third challenge: maintaining an effective communication system that allows couples to share their deepest feelings, joys, and concerns.

OPEN IN PRAYER (1 minute)

God, we thank you for giving us the ability to share intimately with one another. Help us to learn better ways of communicating with each other. Where there are old and perhaps damaging communication patterns, help us to replace them with healthier ones. Help us to desire to share deeply with one another, and to care deeply for one another. Amen.

REVIEW SESSION THREE (1 minute)

During our last time together, we talked about transitioning from a child-focused to a partner-focused relationship. We looked at how our roles and focus change as we reach the empty nest years. We also discussed ways to develop a more personal, companionship marriage. And as couples, we explored ways to develop we-ness in our marriage relationship.

OVERVIEW OF SESSION FOUR (1 minute)

Please turn to page 253. Today's session focuses on communication. Together we will examine:

- Three negative communication patterns
- How to become an interpersonally competent couple
- Seven tips for talking on a more personal level

VIDEO (15 minutes)

In today's session, Dave and Claudia will discuss various communication patterns, emphasizing the importance of developing positive and personal ways of communicating. We will learn about three dysfunctional communication patterns and talk about what goes into meaningful discussion. As the Arps speak, you may want to jot down some notes in the space provided on page 254.

Planning Notes

_____

_____

_____

_____

_____

_____

_____

_____

_____

_____

_____

_____

_____

_____

_____

_____

_____

_____

_____

_____

_____

_____

_____

_____

_____

_____

_____

_____

_____

_____

_____

_____

Session 4

——— ✥ ———

CHALLENGE THREE
MAINTAIN AN EFFECTIVE COMMUNICATION SYSTEM
THAT ALLOWS YOU TO EXPRESS YOUR DEEPEST
FEELINGS, JOYS, AND CONCERNS

OVERVIEW OF THIS SESSION

During this session we will examine:

- Three negative communication patterns

- How to become an interpersonally competent couple

- Seven tips for talking on a more personal level

——— ✥ ———

253

VIDEO CLIP NOTES

Three negative communication patterns:

1. Avoider-confronter:
2. Conflict-avoiding:
3. Conflict-confronting:

How much of the message is:

Words	(7 percent)
Tone	(38 percent)
Nonverbal	(55 percent)

> Show the video clip for challenge 3.

MARRIAGE FORUM (5 minutes)

Please turn to page 255. During the video, Dave and Claudia showed us some animals that represented the negative ways in which some couples communicate. Did you identify with any of the Arps' animal friends? What about the communication patterns they discussed? Why do you think the first three communication patterns would not be productive?

> Allow time for people to respond.

If someone is basically an avoider, what can that person do to be more assertive and up front with his or her feelings?

> Allow time for people to respond.

What do you think a confrontive person could do to encourage his or her partner to be more comfortable about sharing thoughts and feelings on a deeper level?

> Allow time for people to respond.

MY REFLECTION TIME (5 minutes)

Please look at page 255. Take about five minutes to individually answer the questions there, regarding (1) what you believe your typical pattern of communication is, and (2) what you believe your spouse's typical pattern of communication is. Briefly write your responses.

> After 4 minutes have elapsed, give your group a 1-minute warning before moving on to the next segment.

ONE ON ONE (5 minutes)

Now break into your one-on-one groups and share your responses with your partner.

Planning Notes

_____

_____

_____

_____

_____

_____

_____

_____

_____

_____

_____

_____

_____

_____

_____

_____

_____

_____

_____

MARRIAGE FORUM

What animals do you identify with?

Did you identify with any of the communication patterns discussed in the video?

MY REFLECTION TIME

Privately answer the following questions.

What do I believe is my basic pattern of communication?

What do I believe is my spouse's basic pattern of communication?

_____

_____

_____

_____

_____

_____

_____

_____

_____

_____

_____

_____

_____

_____

_____

_____

_____

_____

_____

After 4 minutes have elapsed, give the group a 1-minute warning before going on to the next segment.

MARRIAGE FORUM (10 minutes)

Stay where you are, but let's move into another "Marriage Forum," or large-group discussion. Please turn to page 25. We've talked a little about communication patterns—three of which are not very healthy, especially in the second half of marriage. Now let's focus on the "interpersonally competent" couple. What do you think that means? How would an interpersonally competent couple communicate?

Allow time for people to respond.

How could reading books like *Men Are from Mars; Women Are from Venus* be helpful? Has anyone here read that particular book or one like it? If so, would you give us your impression?

Allow time for people to respond.

Claudia and Dave write that in our culture we tend to "guard our inner thoughts, feelings, and wishes and try to hide our weaknesses. We wear masks in order to hide our real selves." What do you think would make it more comfortable to reveal your real feelings—especially with your spouse?

Allow time for people to respond.

ONE ON ONE (10 minutes)

Please turn to page 258. There you will find the seven tips for talking on a more personal level. Quickly read these over, then complete the self- and spouse-evaluation forms found on pages 258–259. When you've finished, share your evaluations with each other.

After 9 minutes give your group a 1-minute warning before continuing on to the last segment of this session.

Planning Notes

_____
_____
_____
_____
_____
_____
_____
_____
_____
_____
_____
_____
_____
_____
_____
_____
_____
_____

MARRIAGE FORUM

Define what it means to be interpersonally competent:

Helpful books to read:

Taking off our masks:

ONE ON ONE

Complete the following evaluations and rate yourself (and then your spouse) from one to five in each category, with one indicating no skill and five indicating a high level of skill.

Communication Skills, Self-Evaluation

Skills taken from the seven tips for talking on a more personal level

	1 No Skill	2 Little Skill	3 Average Skill	4 Good Skill	5 High Skill
Listen without interrupting	1	2	3	4	5
Clue into nonverbal messages	1	2	3	4	5
Communicate both positive and negative feelings easily	1	2	3	4	5
Use "I" statements, rather than more accusatory "you" statements or "why" questions	1	2	3	4	5
Employ mirroring skills so as to complete the communication cycle	1	2	3	4	5
Neither attack nor defend	1	2	3	4	5
Regularly communicate or touch base	1	2	3	4	5

Communication Skills, Spouse-Evaluation

Skills taken from the seven tips for talking on a more personal level

	1 No Skill	2 Little Skill	3 Average Skill	4 Good Skill	5 High Skill
Listen without interrupting	1	2	3	4	5
Clue into nonverbal messages	1	2	3	4	5
Communicate both positive and negative feelings easily	1	2	3	4	5
Use "I" statements, rather than more accusatory "you" statements or "why" questions	1	2	3	4	5
Employ mirroring skills so as to complete the communication cycle	1	2	3	4	5
Neither attack nor defend	1	2	3	4	5
Regularly communicate or touch base	1	2	3	4	5

WRAP-UP

Assignments for next session:

1. Complete the Marriage Builders on pages 100, 101, and 102.

WRAP-UP (5 minutes)

If nothing else, the last exercise you did should give you something to talk about this week! Building good communication skills takes time, but Dave and Claudia assure us that the time taken is well worth the effort.

So that you can continue to build good communication skills, please turn to pages 100 and 101. These two Marriage Builders will help you express both positive and negative feelings, using "I" statements. I encourage you to take the time to complete these exercises and then practice verbalizing your positive and negative feelings—remembering that it takes five positive statements to overcome one negative statement.

Now turn to page 102. Complete this Marriage Builder individually with the idea that you will make a date and go over the results of this exercise together.

Before we meet again, please read the chapter titled "Challenge Four: Use Anger and Conflict in a Creative Way to Build Your Relationship," which begins on page 103.

Close in Prayer

Father, this week as we begin to develop healthy communication skills, help us to be open, honest, willing to listen, and able to respond. Breaking old habits is hard, but with your help we know we can succeed. I pray for each couple here, that their relationship will become more meaningful this week. Honor the desires of our hearts to grow in love and intimacy with each other—and with you. Amen.

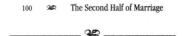

100   The Second Half of Marriage

MARRIAGE BUILDER

Expressing Positive Feelings

Since it is not easy for some to communicate feelings, begin by brainstorming positive feelings words. Then it is easier to form them into encouraging statements. Here are some words to get you started:

"I feel ..."

happy	optimistic
excited	enthusiastic
joyful	pleased
content	encouraged
relaxed	creative
grateful	calm
loved	secure
confident	

Now think about all the positive things about your mate and write them into encouraging sentences, using feelings words. (For example, "I am *relaxed* when I am in your presence" or "I feel *secure* when I am in your arms" or "I am *encouraged* when you give me your undivided attention.")

Next, look for opportunities to verbalize your positive feelings to your mate!

Challenge Three   101

MARRIAGE BUILDER

Expressing Negative Feelings

Since we have difficulty communicating anger in a positive way, begin by brainstorming negative feelings words. Then it is easier to form them into statements that are helpful and do not blame or attack the other person. Here are some words to get you started:

"I feel ..."

hurt	sad	uneasy
frustrated	trapped	embarrassed
angry	squelched	anxious
threatened	scared	belittled
lonely	afraid	used
confused	pressured	attacked
stressed	crushed	irritated
depressed	ignored	tense

Now think of a couple of situations in which you would like to be able to express your negative feelings, but express them in a positive way. Write out what you would like to say, using feelings words and without attacking or blaming your spouse. Remember to start your sentences with "I." (For example, "I feel *anxious* when we don't talk through our budget and decide together how to spend our money" or "I feel *frustrated* when we spend most of our time talking about our children and their problems" or "I am *fearful* that we aren't adequately preparing for retirement.")

---

102   The Second Half of Marriage

MARRIAGE BUILDER

"Can We Talk about It?"

Make a list of topics for discussion:

1. Topics I would like to talk about:

2. Topics I think my mate would like to talk about:

3. Topics I'm not ready to talk about right now. Let's wait on these:

Challenge Four

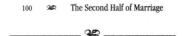

Use Anger and Conflict in a Creative Way to Build Your Relationship

Session 5: Challenge Four

USE ANGER AND CONFLICT IN A CREATIVE WAY TO BUILD YOUR RELATIONSHIP

LEADER PREPARATION

Just as there is turbulence when it comes to air travel, there is also turbulence in marriage. It is inevitable. Claudia and Dave write, "The only way to avoid turbulence in marriage is to stay on the ground and go nowhere."

Couples may handle the light and moderate turbulence with relative ease—sometimes even with humor; however, it's the severe and extreme turbulence that couples find most difficult. Often stress can cause turbulence—and even if the situation is relatively minor, stress can make it seem worse. Hectic schedules, chronic health conditions, or an accumulation of smaller issues can put any marriage on overload.

Conflict and anger are givens in any marriage, but if we learn skills for dealing with them—processing our anger and arguing in a constructive, positive way—we can build rather than destroy our relationship. Dave and Claudia urge couples to learn how to process their anger in healthy ways. They remind us that anger is a secondary reaction to either fear or frustration, so they offer the following suggestions for when we realize that we're becoming angry.

- *Analyze your own anger.* Ask yourself, "What am I really angry about? What is the problem, and whose problem is it? How can I sort out who is responsible for what? How can I learn to express my anger in a way that will not leave me feeling helpless and powerless? How can I clearly communicate my position without becoming defensive or attacking? What risks and losses might I face if I become clearer and more assertive?" Once you understand your own negative feelings, you can learn skills for expressing them in a way that is not attacking.
- *Together as a couple make an anger contract.* This is a proactive way to confront anger as a couple. Make your anger contract at a time when you are not angry!

Planning Notes

_____
_____
_____
_____
_____
_____
_____
_____
_____
_____
_____
_____
_____
_____
_____
_____
_____
_____
_____
_____
_____
_____
_____
_____
_____
_____
_____
_____
_____
_____
_____
_____
_____
_____
_____

First, agree to tell each other when you first realize you are getting angry. Second, renounce the "right" to vent your anger on your spouse. Third, ask for your spouse's help in dealing with whatever is causing the anger. This will help you resist attacking each other or becoming defensive. Dave and Claudia remind us, "The reason it is important to deal with angry feelings is that in most conflicts, it isn't the facts that are bothering us, it's the strong negative feelings. Once those feelings are diffused and processed, it's simple to work at resolving the conflict."

Dave and Claudia recommend a four-step process to resolving conflicts.

1. *State the problem.* Write it out, if necessary, to clarify what the problem really is.
2. *Identify what is at stake and what each has invested.* Who has the greater need for a solution?
3. *List possible solutions.* Be creative and list as many as you can—including humorous ones to lighten the mood.
4. *Choose one and try it.* If the one you choose doesn't work, try another.

The Arps have found that most issues are resolved in one of three ways.

1. *A gift of love* to the one who needs it the most.
2. *Compromise.* Each person gives a little in order to meet somewhere in the middle.
3. *Agree to disagree.* Sometimes there is no simple solution. Each has his or her own opinions. It's at times like this when it's best to agree to disagree.

Marriage turbulence can even be healthy! A solid marriage relationship provides "a safe place to resolve honest conflict and process your anger. It can help your marriage grow."

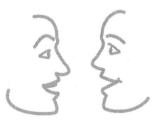

WELCOME (1 minute)

Call the group together and welcome them to session 5, in which they will discuss the fourth challenge as described in *The Second Half of Marriage.* Tell your group that today's challenge focuses on creatively using anger and conflict to build a solid relationship.

Planning Notes

_____

_____

_____

_____

_____

_____

_____

_____

_____

_____

_____

_____

_____

_____

_____

_____

_____

_____

_____

_____

_____

_____

_____

_____

_____

_____

_____

_____

_____

_____

_____

_____

_____

_____

OPEN IN PRAYER (1 minute)

Father, as we discuss the whole idea of anger and conflict, help us to remember that you are the creator of our emotions and that anger can serve to make us stronger, both individually and as a couple, if we harness it and look for ways to resolve our conflicts creatively. And as we seek to build our relationship with our spouse, we ask that you would guard our hearts, minds, and words. Amen.

REVIEW SESSION FOUR (1 minute)

Our last session focused on communication. We learned about three negative communication patterns: avoider-confronter, conflict-avoiding, conflict-confronting. We also discussed how to become an interpersonally competent couple. And we went over the seven tips for talking on a more personal level.

OVERVIEW OF SESSION FIVE (1 minute)

This week we're going to tackle anger and conflicts. Please turn to page 261. In this session we're going to explore:

- How to process anger by making an anger contract
- A four-step process for resolving conflicts
- Three ways in which most conflicts are resolved

VIDEO (15 minutes)

In this clip, Dave and Claudia will discuss ways to deal with anger and conflict that will actually help build the relationship. They will share some personal stories and how abiding by their "anger contract" may have saved their lives. Please feel free to take notes in the space provided on page 262.

> Show the video clip for challenge 4.

MARRIAGE FORUM (10 minutes)

In their book, Dave and Claudia compare marital conflicts to air turbulence. They cite four basic types of turbulence: light, moderate, severe, and extreme. Let's throw out some examples—and they don't necessarily have to be personal examples—of each type of "marital turbulence." I'd like your opinion; what would constitute light turbulence? Turn to page 263 if you'd like to take notes during our discussion.

Planning Notes

_____

_____

_____

_____

_____

_____

_____

_____

_____

_____

_____

_____

_____

_____

_____

_____

Session 5

—— ❧ ——

CHALLENGE FOUR
USE ANGER AND CONFLICT IN A CREATIVE WAY TO BUILD YOUR RELATIONSHIP

OVERVIEW OF THIS SESSION

During this session we will explore:

- How to process anger by making an anger contract

- A four-step process for resolving conflicts

- Three ways in which most conflicts are resolved

—— ❧ ——

261

VIDEO CLIP NOTES

MARRIAGE FORUM

List examples of four basic types of marital turbulence.

1. Light turbulence

2. Moderate turbulence

3. Severe turbulence

4. Extreme turbulence

> Give the group time to respond.

Now let's give some examples of moderate turbulence.

> Give the group time to respond.

What would be considered severe turbulence, in your opinion?

> Give the group time to respond.

Now, what do you think would constitute extreme turbulence?

> Give the group time to respond.

MY REFLECTION TIME (5 minutes)

When dealing with anger, Dave and Claudia urge spouses to first deal with their own anger as individuals. Please turn to pages 108–109 and read the section titled "First Deal with Your Own Anger," paying special attention to the questions on page 109. Think about how these questions might help you in the future to deal with your own anger.

> After 4 minutes have elapsed, give your group a 1-minute warning before continuing on to the next segment.

ONE ON ONE (10 minutes)

Next we want to break into our one-on-one groups and talk about processing anger as a couple. Part of processing anger is making an "anger contract" *before* you are faced with a conflict. Turn to page 110 and read the contract that David and Vera Mace, the Arps' mentors, wrote. Then turn to page 117 to review the contract Dave and Claudia came up with for themselves. Take a few minutes to discuss the following and take notes on page 264:

- Would an anger contract work for us?
- Can we agree to the three simple terms of the Arps' contract?
- Are we willing to sign and stick to this agreement now? If not, what is standing in the way?

---

108 ❧ The Second Half of Marriage

wishes and rights second. For us that means copiloting, and together setting the course for our marriage.

As Copilots, Agree on Where You're Going

Make sure that as copilots you agree on the direction you're headed. In the second half of marriage, defined roles are fewer and the division of responsibilities is blurred. For a harmonious flight, you need to have a way to come to a consensus when there is a difference of opinion. No longer does "I'll just make the decision" work. With a companionship marriage, you can be partners in piloting your marriage.

IDENTIFYING MARITAL TURBULENCE

Constructive arguing involves expressing negative feelings in a positive way. In the last chapter, we saw that the avoider tends to suppress anger, while the confronter tends to vent it. Both need to learn to express their strong negative feelings in a way that releases positive energy and builds their relationship. It is not unlike learning to speak a new language. They have to learn how to work out their anger as a couple. Only then are couples equipped to take steps to resolve an issue. Let's look closer at how to process anger.

First Deal with Your Own Anger

"That's great," said one wife in a recent Marriage Alive seminar. "I've learned how to express my negative feelings and anger to my husband, Fred, in this way, but he just looks at me and says, 'So what?' What am I supposed to do now?"

"First, deal with your own anger," we told her. "Expressing your negative feelings without attacking your husband is a positive step. However, you may need to analyze your own feelings."

When we have negative feelings, we need to look inward before we can relate outward. Dr. Harriet Lerner, in *The Dance of Anger*, points out, "When emotional intensity is high, many of us engage in nonproductive efforts to change the other person, and in so doing, fail to exercise our power to clarify and change our own selves." She suggests several questions to ask yourself:

Challenge Four ❧ 109

What am I really angry about?

What is the problem and whose problem is it?

How can I sort out who is responsible for what?

How can I learn to express my anger in a way that will not leave me feeling helpless and powerless?

When I am angry, how can I clearly communicate my position without becoming defensive or attacking?

What risks and losses might I face if I become clearer and more assertive?[3]

When dealing with our own anger, remember that, as we stated in challenge 1, we can change no other person by direct action. We can only change ourselves. But an interesting thing happens—when we change our responses, others may change in response to us. Dr. Lerner notes,

We are responsible for our own behavior. But we are not responsible for other people's reactions; nor are they responsible for ours. . . . We begin to use our anger as a vehicle for change when we are able to share our reactions without holding the other person responsible for causing our feelings, and without blaming ourselves for the reactions that other people have in response to our choices and actions.[4]

Processing Anger as a Couple

Once we are aware of our own negative feelings and have some understanding of them, we are ready to confront anger as a couple. We will always be indebted to our mentors, David and Vera Mace, for helping us to handle anger as a couple and to use it as a positive force in our relationship. The Maces suggest that a couple make an anger contract. The greatest problem in marriage is not the lack of communication but the inability to handle and process anger. Anger is a normal, healthy emotion; a person who doesn't get angry is not a normal human being. However, once angry, we are responsible for what we do. Venting anger simply increases the intensity, and suppressing anger is unhealthy. The Maces suggest that a better way is to process anger.

---

110 ❧ The Second Half of Marriage

They made a contract that they activate at the first sign of anger. Here are their three steps, which we've modified and adopted as our own:

1. We agree to acknowledge our anger to each other as soon as we become aware of it.
2. We renounce the right to vent anger at each other. It's OK to say something like, "I'm getting angry with you, but you know I'm not going to attack you." The other person does not have to defend himself. (Remember our agreement in the last chapter that we will not attack each other or defend ourselves? This step reinforces that commitment.)
3. We will each ask for the other's help in dealing with anger that develops. If your partner is angry with you and appeals to you to help clear it up, it is very much in your interest to respond. The Maces suggest forming a coalition. They say, "Our contract commits us to working on each angry situation that develops between us until we clear it up."[5]

We have included a copy of our anger contract for your own personal use at the end of this chapter.

RESOLVING MARITAL TURBULENCE

No one does it all right; the Arps are no exception. The time Dave scratched our door with the clothes bag, Claudia totally forgot we even had an anger contract! But we do remember it most of the time, and that's what makes the difference.

The reason it is important to deal with angry feelings is that in most conflicts, it isn't the facts that are bothering us, it's the strong negative feelings. Once those feelings are diffused and processed, it's simple to work at resolving the conflict. And you don't have to agree on everything. If we agreed on everything, one of us would be unnecessary!

Steps for Resolving Conflict

There are a number of problem-solving formulas, but most contain four steps:

Challenge Four ❧ 117

———— ❧ ————

MARRIAGE BUILDER

Anger Contract

The following can become your own anger contract. Trust us, this is one of the most important contracts you will ever sign.

❧

Whenever one of us becomes angry,

1. we will acknowledge our anger to each other as soon as we become aware of it;
2. we will renounce the right to vent anger at each other or to defend ourselves;
3. we will ask for each other's help in dealing with the anger that has developed.[10]

Signed _____

Signed _____

---

264 ❧ The Second Half of Marriage Participant's Guide

MY REFLECTION TIME

Turn to pages 108–109 and read the section titled "First Deal with Your Own Anger." Think about how the questions on page 109 might help you in the future to deal with your own anger.

ONE ON ONE

Turn to page 110 and read the anger contract David and Vera Mace came up with. Next turn to page 117 and read the contract Dave and Claudia adapted from the Mace's contract. Discuss the following:

• Would an anger contract work for us?

• Can we agree to the three simple terms of the Arps' contract?

• Are we willing to sign and stick to this agreement now? If not, what is standing in the way?

> After 9 minutes have elapsed, give the group a 1-minute warning before moving on to the next section.

MARRIAGE FORUM (10 minutes)

You may stay where you are for this next section. Now we're going to try to help a fictitious couple with a problem they are having, by using the four-step process to resolving conflicts that Dave and Claudia talk about on page 111. Please turn to page 265 and read along with me about Natalie and Greg's latest marital conflict.

Greg and Natalie's Conflict

Natalie has invited Greg's parents over for dinner after church on Sunday. She told Greg about the dinner invitation earlier in the week and asked him if he could help her by carving the turkey. Greg agreed. While fixing dinner, Natalie discovered that she needed some milk, butter, and napkins. She wrote out a quick list, gave it to Greg, and asked if he would pick up these items at the store. He said that he would and took off.

About thirty minutes later Greg's parents arrive for dinner. But Greg still hasn't come back from the store. Dinner is ready; however, Natalie is still waiting for the milk and butter so she can finish making the whipped potatoes. Another thirty minutes go by before Natalie hears the car pull into the driveway. A few minutes later Greg walks in with three bags full of groceries—"deals" he saw while shopping for the three items Natalie had requested.
Natalie is upset that dinner has been delayed and that Greg purchased items not on the list. Greg is sorry that he's late but can't understand why Natalie would be upset that he bought extra items on sale.

Now, turn to pages 265–266 and take notes, if you wish, while we discuss this scenario.

How is Natalie feeling? Is Greg surprised at her reaction?

> Give the group time to respond.

Before Natalie and Greg can resolve this issue, they each need to deal with their own anger. What would Natalie say if they had an anger contract? What if they had no anger contract—what might her response be?

> Give the group time to respond.

Planning Notes

_____

_____

_____

_____

_____

_____

_____

_____

_____

_____

_____

_____

_____

_____

_____

_____

_____

---

1. State the problem. Too often couples try to resolve conflict without agreeing on what the conflict really is! We find it helpful to write it out so that we're both trying to resolve the same thing.

2. Identify what is at stake and what each has invested. Who has the greatest need for a solution? When Claudia was less satisfied than Dave about the division of labor in our home, Claudia felt the greatest need for a solution!

3. List possible solutions. The more the merrier. We brainstorm and think of as many solutions as possible. And remember, adding humor will relieve stress and lighten up any situation.

4. Choose one and try it! If your first choice doesn't work, don't give up. Check your list and try another possible solution and then another until something works. Over the years as we have searched for solutions for our own issues and have helped other couples work through theirs, a pattern seemed to develop. Most issues are resolved in one of three ways.

The first way is to give a gift of love. We ask if whatever we are talking about is more important to one than to the other. Then the one to whom it is less important may simply agree to give in and give a gift of love. The Scriptures tell us it is more blessed to give than to receive, and this is certainly true in marriage—unless it's one person who is doing all of the giving, and then you have another problem!

The second way to find resolution is to compromise—for each to give a little; to meet somewhere in the middle. Many times we compromise. There are other times when we simply agree to disagree, and that's the third way to settle an issue. Some things aren't that important, and as we said, we don't need to agree on everything. We agree with Ray Ortlund: "Why do we have to agree, or win, or conclude every discussion? Some great truths are opposites and must forever be held in tension."[6]

At times we like to debate. (Let's clarify that: Claudia likes to debate. For Dave, debating with Claudia is a gift of love.) It can be intellectually stimulating to have differing views. A little turbulence can be healthy for the second half of marriage.

MARRIAGE FORUM

Greg and Natalie's Conflict

Natalie has invited Greg's parents over for dinner after church on Sunday. She told Greg about the dinner invitation earlier in the week and asked him if he could help her by carving the turkey. Greg agreed. While fixing dinner, Natalie discovered that she needed some milk, butter, and napkins. She wrote out a quick list, gave it to Greg, and asked if he would pick up these items at the store. He said that he would and took off.

About thirty minutes later Greg's parents arrive for dinner. But Greg still hasn't come back from the store. Dinner is ready; however, Natalie is still waiting for the milk and butter so she can finish making the whipped potatoes. Another thirty minutes go by before Natalie hears the car pull into the driveway. A few minutes later Greg walks in with three bags full of groceries—"deals" he saw while shopping for the three items Natalie had requested. Natalie is upset that dinner has been delayed and that Greg purchased items not on the list. Greg is sorry that he's late but can't understand why Natalie would be upset that he bought extra items on sale.

How is Natalie feeling? Is Greg surprised at her reaction?

ONE ON ONE

Discuss your answers with your partner.
Cite examples to support your answers.

Let's do the same exercise for Greg. What would his response be if he were abiding by an anger contract? Or just responding naturally?

Give the group time to respond.

Now let's define the conflict and apply the four steps Dave and Claudia recommend to resolving a conflict. The most critical step is identifying the problem. Too many couples try to resolve a conflict before they clearly identify the issue and how each person feels about it.

What is the problem?

Give the group time to respond.

What exactly is at stake here? Who has the greater need to reach a solution?

Give the group time to respond.

Come up with some possible solutions.

Give the group time to respond.

The fourth step would be for Greg and Natalie to choose one of these solutions and try it out.

Dave and Claudia suggest that issues are usually resolved in one of three ways: a gift of love, compromise, agree to disagree.

What gift of love could Greg give to Natalie?

Give the group time to respond.

What gift of love could Natalie give to Greg?

Give the group time to respond.

How could they compromise?

Give the group time to respond.

Give examples of why they may have to agree to disagree.

Give the group time to respond.

Planning Notes

WRAP-UP (5 minutes)

It's easier to come up with solutions for other people's problems. The real test will be for us to apply these steps to our own conflicts as they arise. To make this practical to us as couples, please turn to page 115. There you will find a Marriage Builder titled "Dealing with Marital Turbulence." I strongly encourage each of you to take a serious look at this exercise. Whether you do it first individually and then discuss it together or do it as a couple, this Marriage Builder can help you develop good conflict-resolution skills that can build your relationship.

The Marriage Builder on page 116 should be done individually but discussed with your spouse, if at all possible. This exercise will help you to identify ways in which you express your own anger.

If you did not already sign the anger contract on page 117, I encourage to do so. Again, if one or both of you are not willing to sign it, you need to identify why and work on resolving that issue first.

Before we meet again, please read the chapter titled "Challenge Five: Build a Deeper Friendship and Enjoy Your Spouse," which begins on page 119.

Close in Prayer

Heavenly Father, we have started to look deep within ourselves and examine how we handle our anger toward each other. Father, help us to forgive one another and put our marriage first and our personal wishes and rights second. Whenever possible, help us to willingly give the gift of love, compromise, or agree to disagree when we encounter marital turbulence. Help us to preserve the relationship and incur no structural damage to our marriage. Thank you that we can use conflict and anger in a creative way to build a better relationship. Amen.

---✦---

MARRIAGE BUILDER

Dealing With Marital Turbulence

You can do this exercise alone or as a couple. If you are doing it alone, first go through the list of questions and answer them for yourself. Then go through it a second time and answer them the way you think your spouse would answer. Seek to see things from his or her perspective, and it can benefit your relationship.

Part One: Identifying Areas of Marital Turbulence

List possible areas:

Rate each area: light, moderate, severe, extreme

Part Two: Identifying My Style

I usually resolve conflict by:
___giving gifts of love
___giving a little to find a solution
___agreeing to disagree
___other

What I would like to do in the future:

Part Three: Is There Presently an Issue That Needs to Be Resolved?

Can I express my negative feelings in a positive way, without blaming or attacking?

Is there some way I can diffuse the anger?

Is there a way to resolve the issue?
___give gift of love
___compromise
___agree to disagree

---✦---

MARRIAGE BUILDER

Processing Our Anger

Consider the following questions. If possible, discuss with your mate.

How do you currently handle anger?

How would you like to handle anger?

Are you willing to sign the anger contract?

---✦---

MARRIAGE BUILDER

Anger Contract

The following can become your own anger contract. Trust us, this is one of the most important contracts you will ever sign.

Whenever one of us becomes angry,

1. we will acknowledge our anger to each other as soon as we become aware of it;
2. we will renounce the right to vent anger at each other or to defend ourselves;
3. we will ask for each other's help in dealing with the anger that has developed.[10]

Signed _____
Signed _____

Challenge Five

✦

Build a Deeper Friendship and Enjoy Your Spouse

Session 6: Challenge Five

BUILD A DEEPER FRIENDSHIP AND ENJOY YOUR SPOUSE

LEADER PREPARATION

In this session our focus will be on building a deeper friendship with our spouse, having some fun, and maintaining a good sense of humor. We will also look at what we can do to maintain a healthy lifestyle.

Dave and Claudia write, "An important part of friendship in the second half of marriage is simply spending time together. Remember, a companionship marriage is one in which you put the other person first and your marriage before both of you."

Using comments from participants in their survey and in their Marriage Alive seminars, Dave and Claudia compiled a list of ways in which other couples have fun. Some of them include:

- Taking back roads, getting lost, and then finding the way home again
- Cooking together
- Berry picking
- Organic gardening
- Sailing
- Keeping grandchildren—one at a time
- Having a standing Saturday date to do errands together
- Rocking on the double rocker on the porch

Building a long-term friendship in the second half of life is influenced by health issues. It's easier to build our friendship when we're taking care of our bodies. Dave and Claudia share six ways in which to live a more balanced and healthy life.

1. *Take care of yourself.* An investment in your health is an investment in your friendship with your spouse.
2. *Pace yourself.* Is it realistic to try to maintain the same pace you did ten years ago?

Planning Notes

_____

_____

_____

_____

_____

_____

_____

_____

_____

_____

_____

_____

_____

_____

_____

_____

_____

_____

_____

_____

_____

_____

_____

_____

_____

_____

_____

_____

_____

_____

_____

3. *Build relationships and maintain them.* Building friendships outside your extended family is critical to maintaining a good support system.

4. *Stretch your boundaries.* Try new things or a new approach to "old" things.

5. *Stay involved with life.* Actively search for your passion. Continue to learn and grow.

6. *Hang in there.* Avoid making drastic decisions when you're feeling down. Life is a series of adjustments. Embrace change as a friend.

Through their friendship with Lucy and William, the Arps were reminded "that it takes one heart and one initiator to spice up friendship in a long-term marriage." A conversation with this couple led Dave and Claudia to realize "that praying together and dating your mate have more in common than one would think."

In closing, Dave and Claudia suggest ten fun dates.

1. *Formal-dinner-in-the-park date.* Complete with black tie and evening gown—and a picnic basket!

2. *I'm-too-tired date.* Grab some takeout food, let the answering machine or voice mail get your calls, and relax.

3. *Photo date.* Take pictures of each other and/or set the timer on your camera and take some pictures of yourselves as a couple. (The new picture on the Arps book *The Second Half of Marriage* and on this video resource is from one of their impromptu photo dates.)

4. *Gourmet-cooking date.* Plan the menu, do the shopping, and cook the dinner—together!

5. *Yellow-road-blue-highway date.* Go exploring within a fifty-mile radius of your home, but no fast foods or four-lane highways.

6. *Workout date.* Together work out at a health club or simply take a walk together.

7. *Home Depot date.* Go to a home improvement store and plan and scheme your next home improvement project.

8. *Window-shopping date.* Go window-shopping. If you go when the stores are closed, it will be a cheap date. For a new twist, pick out all the things you have already and make it a "grateful date."

9. *Airport date.* Sit in the air terminal and watch the people come and go. Pretend you're saying good-bye or saying hello and hug and kiss passionately!

10. *Proposal date.* Go to a public place and ask your mate to marry you again.

Planning Notes

WELCOME (1 minute)

> Call the group together and welcome them to session 6. Tell them you will be discussing challenge 5: building a deeper friendship and enjoying your spouse. Be enthusiastic as you approach today's session, as this is when the fun begins!

OPEN IN PRAYER (1 minute)

Dear Father, this last week we had some pretty heavy topics to discuss— dealing with anger and resolving conflicts. And while this is a critical area in building a healthy relationship, we are so grateful that we can also have fun as a couple. Help us to be creative, spontaneous, and open to simply enjoying each other. Amen.

REVIEW SESSION FIVE (1 minute)

During our last time together we took a hard look at anger and conflicts. We talked about how to make an anger contract and process anger in a positive way. We explored the four basic steps to resolving conflicts, and we focused on three specific ways in which most conflicts are resolved: giving a gift of love, compromising, or agreeing to disagree.

OVERVIEW OF SESSION SIX (1 minute)

Please turn to page 269. During this session we are going to delve into:

- Ways in which we can deepen our friendship and have fun together
- The importance of maintaining a healthy and balanced lifestyle
- Fun dates to energize our marriage in the empty-nest years

VIDEO (11 minutes)

Today's video focuses on the dating side of a couple's relationship and reasons why maintaining health and balance are important. Please turn to page 270, where you will find space to take notes.

> Show the video clip for challenge 5.

Planning Notes

_____
_____
_____
_____
_____
_____
_____
_____
_____
_____
_____
_____
_____
_____
_____

Session 6

❧

CHALLENGE FIVE
BUILD A DEEPER FRIENDSHIP AND
ENJOY YOUR SPOUSE

OVERVIEW OF THIS SESSION

Today we will focus on:

• Ways in which we can deepen our friendship and have fun together

• The importance of maintaining a healthy and balanced lifestyle

• Fun dates to energize our marriage in the empty nest years

❧

269

Planning Notes

_____
_____
_____
_____
_____
_____
_____
_____
_____
_____
_____
_____
_____
_____
_____

---

270 ❧ The Second Half of Marriage Participant's Guide

VIDEO CLIP NOTES

MARRIAGE FORUM (10 minutes)

Please turn to pages 123–124. Under the subhead "Just for Fun" you will find responses from couples who either took the Arps' survey or attended a Marriage Alive seminar. Let's read through the ones listed:

- "We like to take the back roads, get lost, and then find our way home again."
- "We like to cook together. Lately, we've been learning to cook Chinese."
- "We pick berries together."
- "We do organic gardening."
- "We learned to sail together."
- "We enjoy keeping our grandchildren—one child at a time."
- "On Saturday morning we have a standing date to run errands together."
- "We like to rock in our double rocker on our screened porch."
- "One night we slept out on our balcony under the stars."
- "Occasionally for long trips we like to drive instead of fly."
- "We like to read aloud together."
- "When we miss our grandchildren, we borrow small children for an evening."
- "From time to time we like to pull out the family albums, slides, videos, and reminisce."
- "On our twenty-fifth wedding anniversary, we made a list of twenty-five things we wanted to do. Then we did them!"
- "We've recently learned how to use E-mail and now stay in better contact with our children."

Now let's hear some things you have done in the past—perhaps even early in your marriage—that were fun. If someone else comes up with an idea that sounds fun, jot it down in the space provided on page 271.

Allow couples time to respond. After 10 minutes have elapsed, begin the next segment.

Planning Notes

_____

_____

_____

_____

_____

_____

_____

_____

_____

_____

_____

_____

_____

_____

_____

_____

_____

_____

_____

Challenge Five 〜 123

GETTING STARTED

An important part of friendship in the second half of marriage is simply spending time together. Remember, a companionship marriage is one in which you put the other person first and your marriage before both of you. That assumes you are spending time together. Daily we have the opportunity to encourage each other and to build our friendship. But we must be intentional about it!

According to psychologists Richard Matterson and Janis Long Harris, "the key to a stronger friendship—and a more satisfying marriage—is developing new habits."[2] What new habits would you like to develop with your mate? How can you stretch your present friendship boundaries?

Matterson and Harris also point out that we have different friendship styles: "Men value *doing* things together, while women value *talking* together. For that reason, shared activities and regular times to talk go hand in hand, allowing the friendship needs of each spouse to be met."[3]

JUST FOR FUN

From our survey and our Marriage Alive seminar participants, we gathered information on what couples who are best friends are doing for fun. Here are some of their responses (note that all contain the two required elements of talking and doing):

"We like to take the back roads, get lost, and then find our way home again."

"We like to cook together. Lately, we've been learning to cook Chinese."

"We pick berries together."

"We do organic gardening."

"We learned to sail together."

"We enjoy keeping our grandchildren—one child at a time."

"On Saturday morning we have a standing date to run errands together."

"We like to rock in our double rocker on our screened porch."

---

124 〜 The Second Half of Marriage

"One night we slept out on our balcony under the stars."

"Occasionally we like to drive instead of fly for long trips."

"We like to read aloud together."

"When we miss our grandchildren, we borrow small children for an evening."

"From time to time we like to pull out the family albums, slides, videos, and reminisce."

"On our twenty-fifth wedding anniversary, we made a list of twenty-five things we wanted to do. Then we did them!"

"We've recently learned how to use E-mail and now stay in better contact with our children."

Make your own fun list of things you can do that include both talking and activity. For a guide, use the Marriage Builder at the end of this chapter.

BUT MY BACK HURTS!

Building a long-term friendship is much easier if it can be experienced with the backdrop of a healthy body. It is definitely easier to maintain that friendship when we also maintain our health.

From our survey, by far the greatest fears that spouses have for the future were related to health concerns—either for themselves or their spouse. Of those in the survey ages fifty and over, 59 percent said that the thing they feared most was death and/or illness, compared with only 19.5 percent of those under fifty.

Many of us find the approach of the second half of life particularly disorienting. Some have a negative attitude, like the husband who said, "Just around the corner, I'm going to lose my hair, my hearing will go, then my eyes, and my sex drive, and then I'll just roll over and die."

Wait a minute! Life doesn't have to be so negative, especially if we take care of ourselves. Why is it that around midlife, our eyesight, backs, and hearing start to go? Shouldn't the extra pounds we gain help fortify us with good health? But the opposite seems to be true. Since health and lifestyle issues are so important to our marriage in the sec-

---

Session 6 〜 271

MARRIAGE FORUM

"Just for Fun" list (See pages 123–124.)

_____

_____

_____

_____

_____

_____

_____

_____

_____

_____

_____

_____

_____

_____

_____

_____

_____

_____

_____

_____

_____

_____

MY REFLECTION TIME (7 minutes)

In a few moments we're going to break into our one-on-one groups. Before we do, please turn to page 131 and take a look at the Marriage Builder. As individuals, spend about 7 minutes completing the form. If you need some help getting started, look at the "Memory Joggers" at the bottom of the page. After about 7 minutes, you will have an opportunity to discuss your list with your spouse.

After 6 minutes have elapsed, give your group a 1-minute warning before having them discuss their individual lists with each other.

ONE ON ONE (8 minutes)

Now move into your one-on-one groups and discuss your list with your spouse. Combine your lists, then choose the things you really want to do and the order in which you want to do them. When you get home, put those activities on your home calendar as dates you will go on with each other.

Now let's break into groups.

Once couples are discussing their lists, give them 7 minutes before issuing the final 1-minute warning.

MARRIAGE FORUM (15 minutes)

You may stay where you are for the next section. Now let's discuss some tips for making the second half more enjoyable. Please refer to page 272, where these tips have been summarized for you.

What are some ways in which we can take care of ourselves and invest in our health?

Allow the group a few moments to respond.

Give some examples of pacing yourself. When is your best time of the day? Your worst? How can you ensure that you are at your best during your best time of the day?

Allow the group a few moments to respond.

Planning Notes

_____

_____

_____

_____

_____

_____

_____

_____

_____

_____

_____

_____

_____

_____

_____

_____

_____

_____

_____

_____

_____

_____

_____

_____

_____

_____

_____

_____

_____

_____

_____

_____

_____

_____

🙟

MARRIAGE BUILDER

Just for Fun

Make a list of things you would like to do just for fun with your mate:

1.
2.
3.
4.
5.

If you both make a list, you can combine your lists. Then choose things you want to do, in order of priority. Write them into your planner or calendar.

Memory Joggers:

1. What things do I enjoy doing with my spouse?

2. What did we enjoy doing together in the past?

3. Which of those previous activities would I still like to do?

4. What would I like for us to do together in the future?

MY REFLECTION TIME

Turn to page 131 and individually complete the Marriage Builder. If you need some help getting started, look at the "Memory Joggers" at the bottom of the page.

ONE ON ONE

Discuss your list with your spouse. Combine your lists, then choose the things you really want to do and prioritize them.

MARRIAGE FORUM

Below is a summary of the six tips for making the second half more enjoyable, which we will discuss as a large group.

1. *Take care of yourself.* Invest in your health.
2. *Pace yourself.* What are your best times of the day? Your worst? How can you ensure that you are at your best during your best time of the day?
3. *Build relationships and maintain them.* Why are friendships outside your family important? What are ways in which you can establish or maintain the friendships you have?
4. *Stretch your boundaries.* What comes to mind when you think of "stretching your boundaries"?
5. *Stay involved with life.* Think about your passions—the things you want to pursue. What are some ways in which you can stay involved with life?
6. *Hang in there.* Life is a series of adjustments. Embrace change as a friend.

Why are friendships outside your own immediate or extended family important? What can you do to establish friendships or maintain the ones you have?

> Allow the group a few moments to respond.

When Dave and Claudia say "stretch your boundaries," what comes to your mind?

> Allow the group a few moments to respond.

How can couples stay involved with life? What are some things about which you feel passionate and want to pursue?

> Allow the group a few moments to respond.

Suggest ways in which you can hang in there when life throws a curve.

> Allow the group a few moments to respond.

How can you take the initiative and put more fun into your marriage? What are some fun dates you would like to have?

> Allow the group a few moments to respond.

WRAP-UP (5 minutes)

I hope this session has inspired some of you to begin thinking of ways to deepen your relationship with your spouse and develop a true friendship. If you haven't already done so, I strongly recommend you read about Lucy and William on pages 128–129. Their approach to dating and spending meaningful time together may prove to be motivating and inspirational to you as you complete your assignments for this week.

Turn to page 132 of your Participant's Guide. Read over the Marriage Builder titled "Planning a Getaway for Two." This exercise is to be done together as a couple. Be sure to have your planning calendars handy. Your assignment is to plan a special getaway date together, put it on the calendar, make all the necessary arrangements, and then do it!

Also, you might want to check out Dave and Claudia's book *10 Great Dates.* Dating is a wonderful way to add structure so you will keep having fun together and building your friendship.

Planning Notes

_____

_____

_____

_____

_____

_____

_____

_____

_____

_____

_____

_____

_____

_____

_____

_____

---

128 🙠 The Second Half of Marriage

LUCY AND WILLIAM

Recently an old friend reminded us that it takes one heart and one initiator to spice up friendship in a long-term marriage. As we boarded our flight to Atlanta, we were surprised to see Lucy. Since there was an empty seat in our row, Lucy joined us. For the entire flight, we talked about her fifty-year-plus marriage. Lucy was flying to her son's home in California to meet her husband, William, who was returning from Asia, where he had been speaking. William is a retired pastor who really has never retired. His passion is missions, and he still speaks all over the world, plus is an interim pastor in a church. Lucy said that working together as a team in the ministry helped prepare them for the time their children left home. "I didn't fall apart," she said, "and one reason was, we had built our marriage and ministered together." Coming from a very traditional marriage, she sure had some modern ideas for making it work. Here are some of her jewels:

"We have dates as often as we can. We have done this for years! We really enjoy going out to eat with each other. But when our finances and time were limited, I'd pack a picnic lunch, go to William's office, and pick him up. We'd go to a park when the weather was nice. Sometimes we just had our picnic in the car. I'd get him back to the office in time for his afternoon appointments.

"Other things we like to do together are going to concerts, the opera, and plays. Recently William took me to Atlanta to see *Miss Saigon*. We like to travel together—like taking a cruise—which I usually have to initiate, but that's OK with me.

"William has always traveled. I still don't let him leave home without a love note in the pajama pocket. I also put notes in his briefcase. I always want to have the last word from home!

"I also travel and speak at conferences. [That's what she had been doing that weekend.] So wherever we are, when we are apart we call each other every evening. I get kidded about this all the time, with comments like: 'Lucy, has William called yet?' 'Better go on to your room, you'll miss William's call.' People kid me but I think they are envious. After over fifty years of marriage, how many people call each

---

other each night when they are apart? But one night this past weekend, there was no call from William, and my friends really got worried. Then I discovered they had sent the message to the wrong room. I've always called William during the day, just to say hello and that I'm thinking about him. Some say men are not as sentimental, but I know William likes the little things I do.

"I send him cards even when we aren't traveling, just to express my love and appreciation. If the cards don't say exactly what I'm feeling, I just edit them.

"I make William's favorite date cookies, and when he is coming home from a trip, I delight in cooking his favorite meal—scalloped potatoes, meat loaf, green beans, tomato aspic salad, and apple pie. Around the holidays, I always make him a pumpkin pie, and he knows it's a gift of love, because I don't like it and he gets to eat it all!"

"What makes your marriage work besides all the fun?" we asked her.

"I can think of two things," she replied. "First, don't ever put your spouse down in public. If you have a suggestion to make, save it for when you are alone. Second, don't ever go to bed angry. We kneel, hold hands, and pray together when we go to bed at night. It's hard to do that and remain angry. I don't know why it is so hard for couples to pray together, but over the years, it's been the glue that helped us keep it all together."

As we reflected on our conversation with Lucy, we realized that praying together and dating your mate have more in common than one would think. We close this chapter with ten dating suggestions for the second half of marriage.

Ten Fun Dates

1. Formal-dinner-in-the-park date. Put on your black tie and evening gown and grab the picnic basket for an evening under the stars!

2. I'm-just-too-tired date. Order takeout, turn on the answering machine, and just relax and enjoy snuggling while you read or watch a movie.

3. Photo date. Go to your favorite haunt and snap away. Simply set the timer on your camera and run back and smile!

---

132 🙠 The Second Half of Marriage

MARRIAGE BUILDER

Planning a Getaway for Two

1. Brainstorm places you would like to go (make a list and then choose one).

2. Choose possible dates available (choose one and write it down on your calendar; you also may want to choose an alternate date).

3. Designate resources for this weekend (work out a budget; decide if this will be an economy getaway or the big splurge).

4. Make arrangements (pet care, reservations, getting maps, and so on).

5. Make a packing list (don't forget to take along a CD player, candles, matches, reading material, snacks, and so forth).

6. You may want to choose a couple of subjects you would like to talk about.

7. On your way, you may want to take this husband's suggestion: "For entertainment and to stimulate discussion, on long car trips my wife and I like to listen to books-on-tape (Christian speakers, fiction, nonfiction). There's a lot available to buy, and I think you can borrow them inexpensively, if not for free, from most public libraries. It always gets us talking, and time flies!"

For a more detailed guide for a weekend getaway, see our book *The Ultimate Marriage Builder*, from which this planning guide is adapted.[5]

Before we meet again, please read the chapter titled "Challenge Six: Renew Romance and Restore a Pleasurable Sexual Relationship," which begins on page 133.

Close in Prayer

Heavenly Father, help each couple here to plan a meaningful getaway date with each other. Open our minds to be creative and resourceful. Help us to clear our heads and our schedules to make time for each other—and to truly enjoy each other, to put more fun into our relationship, and to enjoy a lasting, deep friendship with each other. Amen.

Planning Notes

_____

_____

_____

_____

_____

_____

_____

_____

_____

_____

_____

_____

_____

_____

_____

_____

_____

Challenge Six

❧

*Renew Romance and Restore a Pleasurable
Sexual Relationship*

133

_____
_____
_____
_____
_____
_____
_____
_____
_____
_____
_____
_____
_____
_____
_____
_____
_____
_____
_____
_____

Session 7: Challenge Six

RENEW ROMANCE AND RESTORE A PLEASURABLE SEXUAL RELATIONSHIP

LEADER PREPARATION

According to Georgia Witkin, Ph.D., clinical professor of psychiatry at Mount Sinai School of Medicine in New York, the hardest part of maintaining love and closeness is "learning how to keep intimacy alive through the years of a marriage—especially the second half."

Marriages grow in stages. In the first decade couples learn about each other. Children come along and test the limits of our energy. The second decade of marriage entails fighting off boredom. But it's the third decade that Dr. Witkin says can be the most dangerous. "Women tend to become more interested in sex, while men become more vulnerable. This is a time to watch out for affairs. But the good news is that if you make it through the third decade, the fourth decade of love can be a renewing time."

Sex is an important aspect of marriage, but it is an area many couples are hesitant to talk about. Where it used to be a taboo subject, particularly among Christians, the subject is finding its way into books, articles, and the media. In one study martial researchers found that sexual activity tends to enhance the health and happiness of the marriage partners.

It's important, as we face the empty nest years, that we reexamine our attitude and bravely talk with our partner about our love life. Also, as we reach midlife and beyond, we need to understand how our bodies change as we age.

As we get older, both men and women experience changes—physically, psychologically, and hormonally. If couples can understand these changes, they can use them to enhance their sexual relationship. In a short article, Edwin Kiester Jr. and Sally Valente Kiester suggest five ways to capitalize on these changes.

1. *Reset the pace.* A man's response time slows down as he ages. Instead of worrying about it, relax and enjoy it. Think of the sexual relationship in the second half as a delightful stroll, not a sprint.

Planning Notes

_____
_____
_____
_____
_____
_____
_____
_____
_____
_____
_____
_____
_____
_____
_____
_____
_____
_____
_____
_____
_____
_____
_____
_____
_____
_____
_____
_____
_____
_____
_____
_____

2. *Take action.* While younger men are stimulated by what they see, by age forty or fifty men are stimulated more by touching and caressing.

3. *Balance the seesaw.* Stop boredom by having both partners be the initiator from time to time. Hormonal changes at this time of life bring couples into closer balance. This can lead to a more compatible love life.

4. *Dare to experiment.* Because a man's response time may be longer, this is a great time in life to experiment. "Remember, getting there can be half the fun."

5. *Achieve more from less.* Find whatever frequency works best for you. Let your lovemaking be anticipated and savored, and make the quality of the sexual experience your focus.

Rekindling romance doesn't just happen. It takes some effort. Couples can read books and talk together about how to "spice up" their love life. The Arps write, "As we work on 'romancing' our own marriage and talk to other couples who are in the second half of marriage, . . . we've discovered several key ingredients for rekindling romance in long-term marriages."

- *Be affectionate.* "Romance isn't reserved just for the young, and neither is it reserved for the bedroom. Being affectionate, thoughtful, and kind at other times will spill over into your love life."

- *Be a listener.* "Your love life may be active, but if it is all action and no talk, you're missing an added dimension of romance. Tell your mate what you like. Use a little body language. Nobody is a mind reader!"

- *Be adventuresome.* "You're only limited by your imagination! Try some variety in when and where you make love."

- *Be playful.* "The empty nest is a great time to enter our second childhood. Too often we take ourselves and our mates too seriously."

- *Be in shape.* "We encourage you to keep physically fit. Walk and exercise for your love life. . . . Not everything is cured by walking and exercise. If you have a medical problem or take medication that interferes with your love life, talk with your physician."

Note: You may occasionally have participants in your group who because of severe health issues, such as prostate cancer, can no longer have sexual intercourse. Their issues are different and often require more in-depth help than this curriculum offers. In some situations medication may help. Encourage consulting with their physician.

Planning Notes

_____
_____
_____
_____
_____
_____
_____
_____
_____
_____
_____
_____
_____
_____
_____
_____
_____
_____
_____
_____
_____
_____
_____
_____
_____
_____
_____
_____
_____
_____
_____
_____
_____
_____
_____
_____
_____
_____
_____

- *Be a little wacky.* "What can you do to jolt your own established patterns? What can you do that is a little out of character?"

And in all things remember to pace yourself. Learn to control your schedule instead of letting it control you. Take time to make your love relationship a priority.

WELCOME (1 minute)

Call the group together and welcome them to session 7, in which the group will examine challenge 6: renewing romance and restoring a pleasurable sexual relationship.

OPEN IN PRAYER (1 minute)

God, today we are going to explore the sexual aspect of our relationship. As we look at ways to renew romance and restore a pleasurable sexual bond, help us to be open and honest with each other. If there are hurts or past disappointments, help us to begin the healing process so we can enjoy our sexual relationship in the way you intended us to. Amen.

REVIEW SESSION SIX (1 minute)

During session 6 we discussed ways in which we can build a deeper friendship and have fun together. We also talked about the importance of maintaining a healthy and balanced lifestyle. Then we looked at some fun dates to energize our marriage.

OVERVIEW OF SESSION SEVEN (1 minute)

Please turn to page 275. Today's session will focus on:

- Enhancing your sexual relationship during the empty nest years
- Understanding the physical, psychological, and hormonal changes at this time of life and how to capitalize on them
- Rekindling romance in your marriage

Planning Notes

_____

_____

_____

_____

_____

_____

_____

_____

_____

_____

_____

_____

_____

_____

_____

_____

_____

Session 7

_____ ✍ _____

CHALLENGE SIX
RENEW ROMANCE AND RESTORE A PLEASURABLE
SEXUAL RELATIONSHIP

OVERVIEW OF THIS SESSION

Today's session will focus on:

- Enhancing your sexual relationship during the empty nest years

- Understanding the physical, psychological, and hormonal changes at this time of life and how to capitalize on them

- Rekindling romance in your marriage

_____ ✍ _____

275

_____

_____

_____

_____

_____

_____

_____

_____

_____

_____

_____

_____

_____

_____

_____

_____

_____

_____

_____

_____

VIDEO (14 minutes)

Please turn to page 276. In today's video clip Dave and Claudia tackle the subject of renewing romance and enjoying each other sexually. They will briefly discuss the first through fourth decades of marriage and then suggest five ways to revitalize our love life as we grow older.

> Show the video clip for challenge 6.

MARRIAGE FORUM (6 minutes)

Please turn to page 277. Let's talk for a few minutes on attitudes toward sex. When you were growing up, how did your parents handle the subject of sex?

> Allow time for people to respond.

When you were first married, what was your attitude about sex? Has your attitude changed over the years? If so, when did your attitude begin to change? What were the circumstances surrounding your change in attitude?

> Allow time for people to respond.

What message should we be sending to our young or adult children about the sexual relationship in marriage? How would you like them to view you?

> Allow time for people to respond.

ONE ON ONE (10 minutes)

In a few moments we're going to break into our one-on-one groups. Right now please turn to page 278. Summarized are the five ways to capitalize on changes people experience as they age. Read these over and then discuss them as they pertain to your relationship. Discuss them in the following context:

- Does this apply to us?
- Has this been a concern to one or both of us?
- How do we, as individuals, feel about this subject?

Planning Notes

_____

_____

_____

_____

_____

_____

_____

_____

_____

_____

_____

_____

_____

_____

_____

_____

_____

VIDEO CLIP NOTES

First decade: discovery years

Second decade: avoid boredom

Third decade: dangerous years

Fourth decade: renewing years

Five ways to capitalize on life changes:

1. Reset the pace
2. Take action
3. Balance the seesaw
4. Dare to experiment
5. Achieve more from less

MARRIAGE FORUM

When you were growing up, how did your parents handle the subject of sex?

When you were first married, what was your attitude about sex? Has your attitude changed over the years? If so, when did your attitude begin to change? What were the circumstances surrounding your change in attitude?

What message should we be sending to our young or adult children about the sexual relationship in marriage? How would you like them to view you?

ONE ON ONE

Summarized are the five ways to capitalize on changes people experience as they age. Read these over and then discuss them as they pertain to your relationship. Discuss them in the following context:

- Does this apply to us?
- Has this been a concern to one or both of us?
- How do we, as individuals, feel about this subject?

1. *Reset the pace.* A man's response time slows down as he ages. Instead of worrying about it, relax and enjoy it. Think of the sexual relationship in the second half as a delightful stroll, not a sprint.
2. *Take action.* While younger men are stimulated by what they see, by age forty or fifty men are stimulated more by touching and caressing.
3. *Balance the seesaw.* Stop boredom by having both partners be the initiator from time to time. Hormonal changes at this time of life can bring couples into closer balance. This can lead to a more compatible love life.
4. *Dare to experiment.* Because a man's response time may be longer, this is a great time in life to experiment. "Remember, getting there can be half the fun."
5. *Achieve more from less.* Find whatever frequency works best for you. Let your lovemaking be anticipated and savored, and make the quality of the sexual experience your focus.

After 9 minutes have elapsed, give couples a 1-minute warning before moving on to the next segment.

MARRIAGE FORUM (15 minutes)

Please turn to page 279. On this page and on pages 144 through 148 there are listed six secrets of rekindling romance. Let's take about 15 minutes to brainstorm these six secrets together, beginning with the first one—be affectionate.

The Arps write, "Romance isn't reserved just for the young, and neither is it reserved for the bedroom. Being affectionate, thoughtful, and kind at other times will spill over into your love life."

What are some ways in which we can show affection and be thoughtful and kind?

Allow time for people to respond.

Another secret to rekindling romance is to be a good listener. Dave and Claudia write, "Your love life may be active, but if it is all action and no talk, you're missing an added dimension of romance. Tell your mate what you like. Use a little body language. Nobody is a mind reader!"

What do you think prevents some couples from communicating? Is it shyness? Distrust? Boredom? What do you think?

Allow time for people to respond.

We're going to combine the next two—be adventuresome and be playful. According to the Arps, "You're only limited by your imagination! Try some variety in when and where you make love. . . . The empty nest is a great time to enter our second childhood. Too often we take ourselves and our mates too seriously."

Do you agree or disagree with these statements? Why?

Allow time for people to respond.

What are some ways in which you think couples could add a little adventure to their love life? How could couples become more playful?

Allow time for people to respond.

MARRIAGE FORUM

Six secrets for rekindling romance:

1. Be affectionate.
2. Be a listener.
3. Be adventuresome.
4. Be playful.
5. Be in shape.
6. Be a little wacky.

ONE ON ONE

Ways in which you would like to rekindle romance in your own marriage:

We also read books and talked about how to spice up our love life. Old habits die hard. If you are a driven workaholic, like us, your love life may suffer. If you've spent the last twenty-five years focusing on your children, it takes work to refocus on your mate. A husband married for twenty-six years responded to our survey with this comment: "The greatest stress in our relationship is sex. My sex drive is overshadowed by my excessive compulsion to succeed in my career. When I get home, I'm just too tired."

At least he was beginning to see the reality of his situation. If you feel like two strangers, it will take effort to get reacquainted. But be encouraged—it can happen if you are willing to work at it.

Since our three months in Europe, things are slowly changing at the Arps'. The emphasis is on the word "slowly." Real change is hard work. It isn't simple to simplify our lives, but we are making progress. We've cut back on our writing schedule. We're planning more times away, times when we leave our work at home. And along the way, we are learning how to put fun and romance back into our relationship.

SIX SECRETS OF REKINDLING ROMANCE

Working on your love life has no age barrier. During one of our Marriage Alive seminars, Elizabeth, who was married for forty years, told us about the struggles in the sexual relationship she shared with her husband: "We were older when we got married. I was twenty-nine and Alfred was thirty-two. We weren't so good in our love life. We tried a number of things that didn't work. I remember reading a book that was supposed to tell us what we needed, and I just wasn't like that. If Alfred had followed that book, he would have been all wrong!

"We were committed to each other, and at one point we gave up watching TV. It was taking up all our free time. As we began to explore different possibilities, I discovered I really liked to cuddle. Then we got a nice stereo system, and that helped put us in the mood and blocked outside noises. Sometimes it's the simple little things that actually made a difference in our love life."

As we work on "romancing" our own marriage and talk to other couples who are in the second half of marriage, like Elizabeth and Alfred, we've discovered several key ingredients for rekindling romance in long-term marriages. Hopefully, they will help you stoke your marital fires.

Be Affectionate

During a "Sweetheart's Banquet" at which we were speaking, an elderly couple came up after our talk, and sheepishly the wife told us, "When we were first married, someone suggested we shower together. We tried it and it was so much fun, we've been showering together every morning since!"

"Now that we aren't so agile," her husband added, "we can steady each other and prevent falls. Plus, after all the years it's still fun to wash each other's hair and backs. The shower is a great place to be affectionate!"

Romance isn't reserved just for the young, and neither is it reserved for the bedroom. Being affectionate, thoughtful, and kind at other times will spill over into your love life. We all like to be nurtured and cherished. Phone calls, notes that say, "I love you," cooking your mate's favorite dish, giving a bouquet of flowers, holding hands, a peck on the cheek, a wink across the room, and saying loving and endearing things to each other will add romance to your relationship.

Be a Listener

Two of the most important lovemaking skills and romance enhancers are listening with your heart and talking to your spouse while you are loving each other. Your love life may be active, but if it is all action and no talk, you're missing an added dimension of romance. Tell your mate what you like. Use a little body language. Nobody is a mind reader!

If you find it difficult to talk about the intimate side of your relationship, start by reading a book together. You may find that this is less threatening, and it may open the door for conversation—and who knows what doors conversation may open! Or use the Marriage Builder at the end of the chapter.

Be Adventuresome

Add some adventure. Try a little spontaneity. If you always make love in the evening, try mornings. Call in late for work and grab a couple of hours with each other while you are fresh. Plan a middle-of-the-day rendezvous. One couple, who both work downtown, took a picnic basket to work and met at a downtown motel on their lunch break. Another couple, on a more austere budget, met during their afternoon break in their car in the parking garage for hugs and kisses. Go on and brainstorm. You're only limited by your imagination! Try some variety in when and where you make love. Remember, variety can be the spice of life. Be explorers.

Be Playful

Our friends Dave and Jeanne love rabbits and have four (the stuffed variety) that always travel with them. When we visited them recently, we personally met their rabbits and discovered rabbit decorating themes all over their house! The rabbits were usually in pairs—just like Dave and Jeanne, who in retirement are usually together. They may be older, but their playful spirit and love of romance has blossomed with years. Romance depends on your attitude and perspective. For instance, Jeanne laughingly said, "What might be considered sexual harassment at work can bring enjoyment and pleasure at home!"

The empty nest is a great time to enter our second childhood. Too often we take ourselves and our mates too seriously. Or we always hurry. Remember, whatever you do to promote romance, getting there is half the fun. Making time for love will help you be good to each other. Take time to unwind from your busy day; make the transition slowly. Go for a walk and hold hands. Stop along the way for a kiss or two. Taking time to kiss and cuddle and laugh and share intimate thoughts during your lovemaking will add romance.

Be in Shape

In our forties, we realized we weren't as agile as we thought. Stress, teenagers, and yard work had taken their toll. This was about the time

---

Claudia injured her back, requiring several months of therapy. Part of her therapy program was to work out with light weights and do numerous exercises. Not only did this benefit her back, it helped her general physical condition so much that Dave decided (under duress) to join her.

Having lived on overload for so long, it seemed strange to take time to work out together. But it has had great benefits—even in the bedroom!

Sometimes romance in the empty nest is zapped by the battle of the bulge. As we age, it's natural—regardless of what the TV ads say—to put on a little padding. Thin may be "in" in our culture, but for the older population, being too thin can be a health hazard. Whatever our scales register, we can improve our fitness and firmness by regular exercise. Fitness walking several times each week gives us energy and helps us stay in shape. Face it, when you feel good about your body, you feel better about romance! So we encourage you to keep physically fit. Walk and exercise for your love life. You won't regret it!

Note: Not everything is cured by walking and exercise. If you have a medical problem or take medication that interferes with your love life, talk with your physician. There may be a simple solution, and it's certainly to your benefit to check it out! A yearly physical is a good investment in the health of your marriage.

Be a Little Wacky

What can you do to jolt your own established patterns? What can you do that is a little out of character? A fun getaway at Shakertown in Kentucky was a little out of character for us. To appreciate this romantic interlude, you need to know your history. Shakertown is basically a museum because the population has totally died out. You see, they practiced celibacy. Each house had separate doors for the women and for the men. Everything was separate. Just walking through the old houses and buildings in the town gave us a real feeling of history. As we stood for some time in the little graveyard, we wondered what kinds of lives those people experienced. Did they have romantic feelings for each other? Did they fall in love? Did they slip away and break the celibacy rules?

Later that evening, as we broke the rules, we thought, *What a great location for empty-nest couples who want to do something creative that is just a little off the wall.* If you live near Kentucky, we recommend Shakertown, but wherever you live, we recommend a weekend getaway. Nothing helps revive romance like focused time away together.

If your budget is limited, be creative. Our friends Joseph and Linda love camping getaways. Other couples trade houses and condos. Maybe you have adult children who would loan you their homes when they are away. When our oldest son and daughter-in-law lived in Williamsburg, Virginia, they offered us their apartment when they were going to be away for several weeks. Imagine our surprise when we arrived to find the table romantically set for two, with candles and their best china! Go on and think creatively. Plan a getaway for yourselves! (See Marriage Builder on page 132 for tips on how to design a weekend getaway.)

LEARN TO PACE YOURSELF

We look forward to growing old together and loving each other along the way, but we are learning that if that is going to happen, we must pace ourselves. We try to control our schedule instead of having it control us, as in our Toronto experience. But there are still times we must fly a lot or make multiple trips. Recently we knew it was time to regroup when we got on the hotel elevator and punched the number for the floor our room was on in the previous city! But even though we still get in hectic situations, we are handling them with a little more savvy. For example, on a recent business trip to Grand Rapids, Michigan, we set our alarm and got up early, and before our long, hectic day of meetings, we took time for us. Making personal time for ourselves before we started made the whole day go better.

The next city, we continued to invest time in us. That Saturday morning in Minneapolis, we took a long walk. We mean a really long walk! As we walked, we talked and forgot how far we were walking. Exhausted but relaxed, we got back to our room about noon to get ready for our afternoon meeting. We had left the "Do not disturb" sign

Planning Notes

_____

_____

_____

_____

_____

_____

_____

Let's address the whole "be in shape" issue. What kind of getting and staying in shape activities could a second half couple share? And let's discuss the physical and psychological benefits while we're at it.

> Allow time for people to respond.

The final suggestion is to be a little wacky. Claudia and Dave ask, "What can you do to jolt your own established patterns? What can you do that is a little out of character?"

Has anyone here ever done anything spontaneously that was out of character? If so, how did it make you feel? Or perhaps you know of someone who did something a little wacky. Watching that person, how did it make you feel?

> Allow time for people to respond.

ONE ON ONE (6 minutes)

Now we are going to break into our one-on-one groups and in light of the previous discussion talk about ways in which you can rekindle romance in your own marriage.

> After 5 minutes have elapsed, give couples a 1-minute warning before moving on to the last segment.

WRAP-UP (5 minutes)

Obviously, rekindling a romance is like rekindling a fire. It can start with a spark and a few twigs. Because this is such an important part of any marriage relationship, I suggest you reread challenge 6 as a couple. Focus on the suggestions you would like to try, and then prioritize them.

If you haven't planned that getaway, I encourage you to do so. That may be the perfect time to have a serious discussion about your relationship and how you want it to look six months from now, one year from now, five years from now.

Now please turn to page 150 and look at the Marriage Builder there. I strongly recommend you use these six questions to help you get started in discussing your sex life. Be frank. Be committed. Be loving.

Before we get together again, please read the chapter titled "Challenge Seven: Adjust to Changing Roles with Aging Parents and Adult Children," which begins on page 151.

Planning Notes

_____

_____

_____

_____

_____

_____

_____

_____

_____

_____

_____

_____

_____

_____

_____

_____

_____

_____

_____

_____

_____

_____

_____

_____

_____

_____

_____

_____

_____

---

150 ❧ The Second Half of Marriage

❧

MARRIAGE BUILDER

Conversation Opener — "Let's Talk about Sex"

1. When you got married, how well prepared were you for the sexual relationship?

2. Did you have any difficulties in the early adjustment period? How well did you deal with these?

3. Were your sexual needs different (for example, in frequency or intensity)?

4. How have you adjusted to your different needs over the years?

5. Has there been a change in your sexual relationship since you moved into the second half of marriage? If so, have you both been able to accept this and adjust to it?

6. What changes would you like to make at the present time?[9]

Challenge Seven

❧

Adjust to Changing Roles with Aging Parents and Adult Children

151

Close in Prayer

Father, we thank you for creating us the way you did. We thank you for the special gift of sex that is ours to cherish in marriage. Help us to show love to each other—to learn to pace ourselves, to stoke our own romantic fires and enjoy this precious gift you have given to us. Amen.

Planning Notes

Session 8: Challenge Seven

ADJUST TO CHANGING ROLES WITH AGING PARENTS AND ADULT CHILDREN

LEADER PREPARATION

Being caught between teenage or adult children and aging parents is a dilemma many second half couples face. The challenge is, how can you keep your marriage the anchor relationship while relating to other family members on both ends of "the family seesaw"?

Dealing with Elderly Parents

Whatever your situation, your relationship with your elderly parents affects your marriage. Whether the effect is positive or negative depends more on you than on the situation. Consider the following typical problems that prevent a healthy relationship with aging parents.

- *Lack of trust.* If parents have little trust and respect for their adult children, it will be hard to have a close relationship. Not all elderly parent–adult children relationships are close. Accepting those things you cannot change will help you to change the things you can.

- *Lack of adult status.* Ever feel as if you're still a kid in your parents' eyes? And that whenever you're around your elderly parents, you react much as you did when you were growing up in their home? You may not be able to change your parents' view of you, but you can make a choice to treat *your* adult children differently.

- *Denial.* Lack of open communication with your aging parents will make helping them more difficult. Also, should memory losses occur and physical changes take place, elderly parents may deny that they need any help. This leaves the adult child in a frustrating place.

Planning Notes

- *Excessive demands and manipulation.* The Arps write, "Along with the demanding parent is the one who is manipulative."

Some biblical truths must be held in tension with each other. On one hand we are told in Genesis 2:24 to leave our parents and cleave to our mate. We need to switch our family allegiance. Yet in the Ten Commandments we are told to honor our mothers and fathers, and this has no expiration date or conditions. But as we honor and care for our parents, we should not put them above our spouse.

Whatever your situation with your parents, try building positive bridges, using one or more of the following suggestions.

- *Collect family history.* Ask your parents questions about their lives when they were younger. Listen to the stories, repeat them, and write them down.
- *Collect family wisdom.* What were all those sayings your mother or father used to utter? Perhaps your parents can even remember some of the things their parents used to say.
- *Make a positive list.* Check out the positive feelings words on page 000 and use them to describe the positive attributes your parents have.
- *Do something out of character.* Even if your parents have never tried a particular activity before, why not suggest doing it if you believe they would enjoy it once they gave it a chance? Be creative in gift giving too.
- *Do something they want to do.* Basically, this is a gift of love. Plan ahead and let them choose an activity—either together as a couple or individually.
- *Provide lots of pictures.* Write the names, dates, and occasions on the backs of pictures and give or send them to your parents in little photo albums. This will help keep them updated on family events. If your parent is on the Internet, sending family pictures is easy to do.

Sometimes there are difficult circumstances to deal with regarding aging parents. The Arps recommend four tips for making whatever you are dealing with less stressful.

1. Deal with false guilt.
2. Don't feel responsible for what you can't control.
3. Get advice from others.
4. Get a life.

Planning Notes

_____

_____

_____

_____

_____

_____

_____

_____

_____

_____

_____

_____

_____

_____

_____

_____

_____

_____

_____

_____

_____

_____

_____

_____

_____

_____

_____

_____

_____

_____

_____

_____

_____

Dealing with Adult Children

"On the other side of the generational seesaw, we face similar issues, but we are the parents!" the Arps write. "The transition into adult relationships with our children and their spouses can be a difficult challenge and if not well managed can greatly affect our own marriage." We need to be willing to let go and respect our adult children's boundaries. An unwillingness to let go is closely related to lack of adult status and lack of trust. The Arps ask, "Are we willing to let go—to release our children into adulthood and let them lead their own lives?"

Building healthy, trusting relationships with your adult children can enrich the second half of your marriage. And when your children marry, develop a relationship with each couple. Visit but don't stay too long. Let them parent their own children. Try not to give advice. Build a relationship with each grandchild.

Whatever your family background and whatever relationship you have today with your own parents, remember that you can build a healthy bridge to your own children and grandchildren. As Dave and Claudia write, "You can pass down to [them] a legacy of healthy family relationships and a marriage model worth following!"

WELCOME (1 minute)

> Call your group together and welcome them to session 8. Explain that they will be looking at challenge 7: adjusting to changing roles with aging parents and adult children. Ask for a show of hands of couples who are dealing with elderly parent issues right now. How many in your group have adult children?

OPEN IN PRAYER (1 minute)

Father, you tell us to honor our parents but also to leave them and cleave to our spouse. As we take a look at a very sensitive area, please help us to do both—honor our parents but also honor our marriage. And on the other side of the seesaw, help us to build positive relationships with our children, and as they transition into adulthood, may we respect their boundaries and enjoy their company. At the same time help us to make time and reserve energy for our marriage, that we may be a model worth following. Amen.

Planning Notes

REVIEW SESSION SEVEN (1 minute)

During our last time together, we took a rather intimate look at the sexual side of our relationship. We discussed life changes—physical, psychological, and hormonal. We discovered ways in which we can use these changes for our benefit in the second half of our marriage. We also examined some ways in which to rekindle romance in our marriage.

OVERVIEW OF SESSION EIGHT (1 minute)

Please turn to page 281. During this session we will take a look at:

- Typical problems that may arise in dealing with elderly parents
- Suggestions for building bridges between us and our aging parents
- Ways to build healthy, trusting relationships with our adult children

VIDEO CLIP (14 minutes)

In today's video clip Dave and Claudia talk about building relationships with our elderly parents and our adult children while at the same time keeping our marriage as the anchor relationship. Please turn to page 282. Feel free to take notes while the video clip is playing.

> Show the video clip for challenge 7.

MARRIAGE FORUM (6 minutes)

Let's discuss some of the intergenerational stresses that typical couples face in the second half of life. How many feel the empty nest is a myth? What are some of the issues you observe in your family and with your friends? Jot down some notes, if you wish, on page 283.

> Give opportunity to respond.

ONE ON ONE (10 minutes)

In a few moments I will have you break into your one-on-one groups. But for right now please look at page 283. There you will find a summary of some typical problems that can arise in your relationship with your aging parents. Discuss each of these potential problems as they relate to you and your parents. Now break into your groups.

Planning Notes

_____

_____

_____

_____

_____

_____

_____

_____

_____

_____

_____

_____

_____

_____

_____

_____

_____

_____

_____

Session 8

❧

CHALLENGE SEVEN
ADJUST TO CHANGING ROLES WITH AGING PARENTS AND ADULT CHILDREN

OVERVIEW OF THIS SESSION

During today's session we will take a look at:

- Typical problems that may arise in dealing with elderly parents
- Suggestions for building bridges between us and our aging parents
- Ways to build healthy, trusting relationships with our adult children

❧

281

VIDEO CLIP NOTES

Tensions between us and our elderly parents:

- Aging parents don't give us adult status
- Unrealistic demands

Tensions between us and our adult children:

- Giving adult status to our adult children
- Setting boundaries

Cast all your anxiety on him because he cares for you.

1 Peter 5:7

When I am afraid, I will trust in you.

Psalm 56:3

_____

_____

_____

_____

_____

_____

_____

_____

_____

MARRIAGE FORUM

Symptoms of intergenerational stress:

ONE ON ONE

Below is a summary of the typical problems that can arise in your relationship with your aging parents. Discuss each of these as they relate to your own personal situation with aging parents.

- *Lack of trust.* Sometimes parents have little trust in their adult children and a lack of respect. This can hamper a close relationship. Realizing that not all elderly parent–adult children relationships are close may help. Also, accepting those things you cannot change will help you to change the things you can.

- *Lack of adult status.* Ever feel as if you're still a kid in your parents' eyes? And that whenever you're around your elderly parents, you react much as you did when you were growing up in their home? You may not be able to change your parents' view of you, but you can make a choice to treat *your* adult children differently.

> After 9 minutes have elapsed, give a 1-minute warning before going on to the next segment.

MARRIAGE FORUM (8 minutes)

Turn to page 284. We have summarized the suggestions for building bridges with your aging parents that can be found on pages 159–161. Let's take the next ten minutes to discuss some of these.

The first one is to collect family history. Do any of you have fathers—or mothers, for that matter—who served in the armed forces? Do any of you have parents who immigrated to this country? Does anyone here have a parent who was once a child? In each person's life there are stories to tell. Name some stories your parents could tell. What have you done to preserve family history?

> Allow a few minutes for people to respond.

The second suggestion is to collect family wisdom. Can anyone here share a favorite saying from a parent—and then explain it?

> Allow a few minutes for people to respond.

Please turn to page 100. There you will find the list of positive feelings words we used to describe our spouse. Will some of you call out some positive words you could use to describe your parents?

> Allow a few minutes for people to respond.

Dave and Claudia recommend we write out several positive sentences about our parents and then use them as we talk with them.

The next suggestion is do something out of character. Who among us has ever surprised our parents with something totally spontaneous and out of character for us? Let's name some ways in which we could add a little sparkle to our parents' lives.

> Allow a few minutes for people to respond.

The last two suggestions entail doing something our parents would like to do and providing lots of pictures. Are there any other ways you can think of—or perhaps you have done—to build a better relationship with your aging parents?

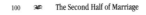

284 ❧ The Second Half of Marriage Participant's Guide

- *Denial.* Lack of open communication with your aging parents will make helping them more difficult. Also, should memory losses occur and physical changes take place, elderly parents may deny that they need any help. This leaves the adult child in a frustrating place.

- *Excessive demands and manipulation.* The Arps write, "Along with the demanding parent is the one who is manipulative."

MARRIAGE FORUM

Below is a summary of some ways in which you can build bridges with your aging parents.

- *Collect family history.* Ask your parents questions about their lives when they were younger. Listen to the stories, repeat them, and write them down.

- *Collect family wisdom.* What were all those sayings your mother or father used to utter? Perhaps your parents can even remember some of the things their parents used to say.

- *Make a positive list.* Check out the positive feelings words on page 100 and use them to describe the positive attributes your parents have.

- *Do something out of character.* Even if your parents have never tried a particular activity before, why not suggest doing it if you believe they would enjoy it once they gave it a chance? Be creative in gift giving too.

- *Do something they want to do.* Basically, this is a gift of love. Plan ahead and let them choose an activity—either together as a couple or individually.

---

100 ❧ The Second Half of Marriage

———— ❧ ————

MARRIAGE BUILDER

Expressing Positive Feelings

Since it is not easy for some to communicate feelings, begin by brainstorming positive feelings words. Then it is easier to form them into encouraging statements. Here are some words to get you started:

"I feel . . ."

happy	optimistic
excited	enthusiastic
joyful	pleased
content	encouraged
relaxed	creative
grateful	calm
loved	secure
confident	

Now think about all the positive things about your mate and write them into encouraging sentences, using feelings words. (For example, "I am *relaxed* when I am in your presence" or "I feel *secure* when I am in your arms" or "I am *encouraged* when you give me your undivided attention.")

Next, look for opportunities to verbalize your positive feelings to your mate!

Challenge Seven ❧ 159

However, this Scripture is not an excuse to withhold care for parents as they age. In the Ten Commandments, we are told to honor our mothers and fathers, and this has no expiration date or conditions. It doesn't say honor your parents until you are twenty-one, nor does it say honor your parents if they deserve it and treat you with respect. In the Scriptures, it is clear that for us as children (even sixty-year-old children), our part of the deal is not dependent on how loving, caring, and understanding our parents are.

THE MARRIAGE BALANCING ACT

At this point we need to refocus. You may want to use the Marriage Builder "Our Needs, Their Needs," at the end of the chapter, to get some perspective on your individual situation. Although we offer a few suggestions, this chapter is not about relating to parents. This is a book about building your marriage for the second half, and you need to continue to invest in your marriage while loving, honoring, and caring for your aging parents. So let's look at what we can do.

Look for the Positive

A saying we repeat often is, "We can do what we can do, and that's what we can do." This may need to become your motto, too, if you want to successfully meet this challenge in the second half of your marriage. Maybe you are blessed with parents who are positive, are in excellent health, and each day look for the best.

Or you may be in a more distressing situation. You may have to look harder to find the positive, but we challenge you to look until you find something. One husband in our survey, who had been married for thirty-four years, wrote that it is all relative: "The empty nest is stressful, but inherently it is not as stressful as raising children." To build positive bridges, consider the following possibilities:

Collect family history. When you are with your parents, sidetrack the "body recital" by asking questions about when they were younger. You may want to take notes or tape record this for family history. Note taking is a good way to occupy your mind, especially when the story being

---

160 ❧ The Second Half of Marriage

told is a repeat. We talk at around one hundred words a minute (older people tend to talk much slower), but we can think at around four hundred words per minute.[2] Because we think faster than we speak, it is harder to listen to the other person, especially if we have already heard about the gall bladder operation numerous times.

Recently one of our sons, in a phone conversation, encouraged his granddad to talk about his experience in World War II. While they talked, he took notes on his computer and then E-mailed the family a little bit of our family history. We remember Dave's grandmother telling us about her first car—the first car in her county—and how she forged streams to get to the next town. We have the blanket she used in that car to cover up her legs to keep warm. Talk about a piece of family history!

Collect family wisdom. Write down sayings that would be interesting to others in the family. Sayings like "I was just born too soon" or "You're as cute as an Indian rubber bouncing ball" help us appreciate the unique characters that our parents are!

Make a positive list. Turn back to the Marriage Builder on page 160 and look at the list of positive feelings words. List things that are positive about your mom and/or dad. Remember, we often forget to express the tender feelings and thoughts we have about our loved ones. As you did with your spouse, write out several positive sentences and then use them the next time you talk to your parent.

Do something out of character. Dave's family was never a "Let's eat out" family, and as his parents aged, they ate out less and less. So when we suggested taking his dad out for a steak dinner to celebrate his eighty-fourth birthday, we were surprised when he enthusiastically agreed. We chose a restaurant he had never been to before even though he has lived in the same city for over thirty years. It was out of character but was a delightful evening for all. Now when we want to give him a special gift, we can give him a gift certificate to that restaurant!

Do something they want to do. Give your elderly parent a gift of love. For Claudia's mother, that could be a shopping trip to Atlanta. But plan ahead. While parents usually like surprises, half of the fun may be the anticipation. Knowing you are coming to visit or are going to call may be as enjoyable as the actual event.

Challenge Seven ❧ 161

Provide lots of pictures. From time to time we will put together little photo albums and send them to our parents. It helps them keep up with grandchildren and great-grandchildren. You may want to do the same. Write the names, the date, and the occasion on the back of each picture. Include the middle name if it happens to be the name of one of your parents. They may have forgotten that a great-grandchild was named after them!

Realize That Life Goes On

You may have heard about the elderly couple who after sixty-five years of marriage went to the lawyer to get a divorce. "Why, after all these years together," the bewildered lawyer asked them, "do you want to get a divorce?"

"Oh," answered the husband, "we were waiting for our children to die."

While no one we know would say they are "waiting for their parents to die," it is possible to put our head in the sand like the ostrich and not face the present and future with objectivity. Whatever your situation with your aging parents, you need to build your own marriage now—not in the future when you have less stress. So take the following four tips:

Deal with false guilt. You simply can't be all things to all people. Remember, you can do what you can do, and that's what you can do.

Don't feel responsible for what you can't control. Anxiety tends to appear when we feel responsible for things we can't control. So remember the prayer used in Alcoholics Anonymous: "God, grant me the serenity to accept the things I cannot change, courage to change the things I can, and wisdom to know the difference." You may even want to make a list of what you can do and can't do.

Get advice from others. Older friends have been a great source of information for us. Observe those with healthy extended family relationships. Ask questions. Read books. Do whatever you can to gather helpful information.

Get a life. Whatever your situation with your aging parents, you need a life of your own. And your marriage needs maintenance, especially in these stressful years.

Allow a few minutes for people to respond.

ONE ON ONE (8 minutes)

In a moment you will break into your one-on-one groups. For now please turn to page 169 and look at the Marriage Builder there. Now, I realize that not all of you have adult children. Some of you, however, will be experiencing that before you know it. For the next eight minutes I want you to complete the Marriage Builder on page 169. If you have adult children, you can evaluate present-day relationships. If you do not have adult children yet, I want you to anticipate their growing up and answer the questions based on how you feel about their growing up and leaving home in the near future. For example, how much contact will you want with your children once they are grown? If you think you are going to be too stifling or not available enough, what can you do to take steps toward changing that now?

Go ahead and break into your couple groups.

After 7 minutes have elapsed, give the group a 1-minute warning before going on to the next segment.

MARRIAGE FORUM (5 minutes)

I would like to spend about five minutes hearing from parents of adult children. Do you have positive relationships with your adult children? Do they live nearby? Do you have grandchildren? If so, what is your relationship with them like? What have you done to ensure a good relationship with your children? What seems to work the best with you?

Solicit responses from people—especially those who you know have grown children.

WRAP-UP (5 minutes)

Balancing a relationship between aging parents, grown-up children, and our own spouse can be a seesaw experience. But being prepared and working out problems as a couple will help you keep your relationship a top priority, yet at the same time allow you to be sensitive to the needs of your family members on either end of the spectrum.

Planning Notes

_____

_____

_____

_____

_____

_____

_____

_____

_____

_____

_____

_____

_____

_____

_____

_____

_____

_____

❧

MARRIAGE BUILDER

Evaluating Your Relationship with Your Adult Children

1. Is the amount of contact you have with your adult children
   a. too little?_____ b. too much?_____ c. about right?_____

   If you would like your answer to be different, what—if anything—can you do about changing it?

2. Do you have a good relationship with your grown children and their spouses?
   If not, is there any way you can make things better?

3. Are you satisfied with the way your grown children relate to you?
   For instance, when you need it, do they offer their help, encouragement, and so on? Do they express appreciation for the ways you help them?

4. Do you do all you can to demonstrate your love, appreciation, and gratitude to your grown children?

5. Do you maintain clear and open communication?

6. If a child of yours has been involved in divorce, have you been able to face the situation with as much understanding and tolerance as possible? If not, what can you do now to strengthen your relationship with your child?[4]

You may need more time to adequately answer the questions in the Marriage Builder on page 169. If you do, please take that time. The more thoroughly you can answer these questions, the better chance you will have of building a healthy, mutually respectful relationship with your adult children.

If you have elderly parents, please complete the Marriage Builder on page 168. You may need to pull out several sheets of paper and do this for each parent involved. People are different—even within the context of marriage—and their needs will be different.

Before we meet again, please read the chapter titled "Challenge Eight: Evaluate Where You Are on Your Spiritual Pilgrimage, Grow Closer to Each Other and to God, and Together Serve Others," which begins on page 287.

Close in Prayer

Heavenly Father, dealing with issues surrounding aging parents and adult children isn't easy. Help us to love them, honor them, respect them, and build solid relationships with them. Even if our relationships weren't good with our parents or with our children, help us to bridge those gaps between us. Help us to be solid in our relationship with our spouse and to provide a godly role model for our children and grandchildren. Amen.

Planning Notes

_____

_____

_____

_____

_____

_____

_____

_____

_____

_____

_____

_____

_____

_____

_____

_____

_____

_____

_____

_____

_____

_____

_____

_____

_____

_____

_____

_____

_____

_____

_____

_____

_____

_____

_____

---

168 ❧ The Second Half of Marriage

--- ❧ ---

MARRIAGE BUILDER

Our Needs, Their Needs

PERSON	NEEDS	HOW MET?		
		Me	Siblings	Other
Parent's present needs				
Our present needs				
Parent's future needs				
Our future needs				

Now think about the following questions. If possible, discuss them with your spouse.

1. What changes need to be made at the present time?

2. What changes will need to be made in the future?

3. What resources do we have to help make these changes (family, friends, other people, agencies, financial, and so forth)?

4. What can we do now to prepare for our future?

Session 9

--- ❧ ---

CHALLENGE EIGHT
EVALUATE WHERE YOU ARE ON YOUR SPIRITUAL PILGRIMAGE, GROW CLOSER TO EACH OTHER AND TO GOD, AND TOGETHER SERVE OTHERS

OVERVIEW OF THIS SESSION

During this session we will explore:

• What a sacred canopy over our marriage means

• Ways to help each other and ourselves along on our spiritual pilgrimage

--- ❧ ---

287

Session 9: Challenge Eight

EVALUATE WHERE YOU ARE ON YOUR SPIRITUAL PILGRIMAGE, GROW CLOSER TO EACH OTHER AND TO GOD, AND TOGETHER SERVE OTHERS

LEADER PREPARATION

In their national survey the Arps observed an alarming trend. "Of the participants (12 percent) who indicated that the best aspect of their marriage was the spiritual aspect, a high percentage of their other responses indicated much dissatisfaction with their marriage."

For example, one husband wrote, "The best aspect of my marriage is putting God first" but then wrote, "The greatest stress in my marriage is too much negative communication and no respect." The Arps write, "It appears that for some, faith and commitment to God is the main reason they are staying in an unhappy marriage."

Dave and Claudia ask, "What's wrong with this picture? Shouldn't our spiritual commitment improve the quality of our marriage? Faith in God should make a radical difference in our relationship with our spouse; it should enhance our love for each other."

The Arps add, "In his book *Spheres of Love*, Stephen G. Post, Ph.D., . . . suggests that the high esteem that marriage once enjoyed has been difficult to sustain because it lacks what he defines as 'a sacred canopy'—an affirmation of the significant foundational beliefs concerning the holy state of marriage.

"Post writes, . . . 'Marriage was part of God's original natural order. Marriage transcends cultures. Marriage is a serious commitment. . . . Marriage is an essentially mysterious union like the mystical one between Christ and the church.'"

Does your marriage have a sacred canopy? The definition of "canopy" includes "a protective covering or shelter from life's storms, a haven, a refuge, a retreat, a sanctuary, a place of safety." When you couple that term with the word "sacred," you add the component of holiness, purity, something set apart or sanctioned.

Planning Notes

What are your basic beliefs about what elevates your own marriage? The Maces, in their book *What's Happening to Clergy Marriages?*, share their core beliefs about their marriage. These beliefs are summarized below.

1. God brought us together in the first place.
2. Our continuing life together is part of God's divine purpose.
3. We have a witness to bear together.
4. A shared life must have a sacrificial quality.
5. A Christian marriage must find spiritual expression.

It is God who can give us new passion for our spouse. He is the one who can enable us to have an open and honest relationship and to construct a sacred marriage canopy over that relationship.

When we talk about the sacred canopy over marriage, the style of the marriage is not the issue. Some marriages are more headship oriented, while others are more partnership oriented. The Maces write that "the Bible gives some support to both the hierarchical and the companionship concepts of marriage." Of far more importance, Dave and Claudia write, is "the quality of the relationship . . . not the form or style."

As each spouse grows in his or her spiritual pilgrimage, the Arps share three suggestions:

1. Accept where both you and your spouse are on that journey.

- Don't force or coerce your spouse to attend or do something with you that you know he or she will not enjoy.
- Be teachable and willing to learn.
- Realize that one of the privileges and joys of a marriage is only having to relate one to one.

2. Promote spiritual closeness and unity through couple devotions and/or prayer together. If you would like to develop the habit of praying together, invest 10 minutes a day.

- Try the 10-minute miracle:

Scripture reading (5 minutes)
One prays (2 minutes)
The other prays (2 minutes)
Silence before the Lord (1 minute)
Monday, Wednesday, Friday the husband takes the lead
Tuesday, Thursday, Saturday the wife takes the lead
Sunday the Lord leads

Planning Notes

3. Together serve others.

- God is the one who gives purpose and meaning to our marriage.
- Reflect his image together in a hurting world.
- Be beacons that give light to others and create a thirst for healthy marriage relationships.

> Note: For this session you may find it helpful to use a whiteboard, chalkboard, or flip chart to record participant responses during the "Marriage Forum" segment.

WELCOME (1 minute)

> Call your group together and welcome them to session 9, in which you will be reviewing the eighth and final challenge: evaluating where you are on your spiritual pilgrimage, growing closer to each other and to God, and together serving others.

OPEN IN PRAYER (1 minute)

Dear Father, today we are going to look at the spiritual dimension of our marriage and how we can grow closer to each other and to you. Open our hearts and eyes to see more clearly what you desire for our marriage, and give us the grace and courage we need to stand strong and make a difference. Amen.

REVIEW SESSION EIGHT (1 minute)

During session 8 we looked at balancing the intergenerational seesaw. We discussed typical problems and ways in which we could build bridges between us and our elderly parents. We also examined ways to build healthy, trusting relationships with our adult children.

OVERVIEW OF SESSION NINE (1 minute)

Please turn to page 287. During this session we will explore:

- What a sacred canopy over our marriage means

Planning Notes

_____

_____

_____

_____

_____

_____

_____

_____

_____

_____

_____

_____

_____

_____

_____

_____

Session 9

——— ✣ ———

CHALLENGE EIGHT

EVALUATE WHERE YOU ARE ON YOUR SPIRITUAL
PILGRIMAGE, GROW CLOSER TO EACH OTHER
AND TO GOD, AND TOGETHER SERVE OTHERS

OVERVIEW OF THIS SESSION

During this session we will explore:

• What a sacred canopy over our marriage means

• Ways to help each other and ourselves along on our spiritual
pilgrimage

——— ✣ ———

287

- Ways to help each other and ourselves along on our spiritual pilgrimage

VIDEO (12 minutes)

In today's video clip Dave and Claudia talk about the sacredness of marriage. They will remind us of three principles from Genesis 2:24: to leave our parents, cleave to one another, and become one flesh. We will also take a look at some ideas for helping us along on our spiritual pilgrimage.

Please turn to page 288, where there is space for you to jot down some notes.

> Show the video clip for challenge 8. Please note that following this clip, there is some promotional information for the Arps' video curriculum *Ten Great Dates to Revitalize Your Marriage.* If couples are interested in continuing with the group, arrange to show it at the end of the last class or at another time. The *Ten Great Dates* series would provide a wonderful follow-up to this study.

MARRIAGE FORUM (14 minutes)

In their book, Dave and Claudia discuss the concept of a "sacred canopy of protection over marriage." Let's discuss the principal words used and try to come up with a definition for this concept. Please turn to page 289, where you can jot some notes.

First of all, let's define the word "sacred."

> Write responses on a whiteboard, chalkboard, or flip chart.

Now let's define the word "canopy." To help us out, I'm going to ask a couple of you to look up some Bible verses and then describe how the word is used.

> Ask for volunteers to look up the following verses. After each reads aloud the verse, ask how the word was used.

Isaiah 4:5–6

Isaiah 40:22

Planning Notes

_____

_____

_____

_____

_____

_____

_____

_____

_____

_____

_____

_____

_____

_____

_____

_____

_____

_____

_____

_____

_____

288 ✇ The Second Half of Marriage Participant's Guide

VIDEO CLIP NOTES

Based on Genesis 2:24:

Leave

Cleave

Become one

_____
_____
_____
_____
_____
_____
_____
_____
_____
_____
_____
_____

_____

_____

_____

_____

_____

_____

_____

_____

_____

_____

_____

_____

_____

_____

_____

_____

_____

_____

_____

_____

_____

Now think about how the word "canopy" is used today. What is the primary purpose of a canopy? Why do you think a canopy is used in the Jewish wedding ceremony?

> Write responses on a whiteboard, chalkboard, or flip chart.

Now let's define the word "marriage." What words come to mind when you think of marriage?

> Write responses on a whiteboard, chalkboard, or flip chart.

Let's put some of these words for "sacred," "canopy," and "marriage" together and come up with a definition.

> Spend the remaining time coming up with one definition; write it on the board.

ONE ON ONE (10 minutes)

In a few moments we will break into our one-on-one groups. For now please turn to page 290. There are five questions that correspond to the core beliefs presented on pages 176 to 177. Take the next ten minutes to answer these questions together. Please break into your one-on-one groups now.

> After 9 minutes have elapsed, give the group a 1-minute warning before moving on to the next segment.

MARRIAGE FORUM (5 minutes)

In the video clip, Dave and Claudia shared three main suggestions about how to grow as a couple on your spiritual pilgrimage. They said to pray together, engage in couple devotions, and together serve others.

In the book, they expound on these three things, which we will discuss in more detail in a few minutes. For now let's share some things we have done to promote spiritual closeness. Are there any particular devotions you have used? Do you pray together regularly? What has proved to be tried and true for some of you? Feel free to take notes during the discussion, using the space provided on page 293.

ONE ON ONE

Below are the Maces' five core beliefs regarding marriage. Read the statements and answer the questions.

1. God brought us together in the first place.

• Do we believe God brought us together?

• How did we first meet?

• What made us so sure that we should be married?

• What ministries are you both interested in?

MARRIAGE FORUM

What things have you done as a couple to promote spiritual closeness?

Are there any particular devotions you have used?

Do you pray together regularly?

What has proved to be tried and true for you?

"holy," "ordained," "sanctioned," "pure," "revered." Certainly all these words describe a truly Christian marriage.

Finally, we studied the word "marriage." And we found terms like "union," "match," "wedlock," "consortium," and "conjugality." If that's all that marriage is, it sure doesn't sound that great!

Then the light went on! It's God's sacred canopy that elevates marriage and makes it a holy institution. Dr. Post reiterates that it is Christianity that provides marriage with the theological roots that make marriage a lifetime commitment in a world that seems incapable of anything more than "limited engagements." "Marriage fails," he writes, "for many reasons, one of which is the lack of a foundation in meanings of any ultimate significance."[3]

Does your marriage have a sacred canopy? What are your basic beliefs about what elevates your marriage? Is your marriage a lifetime commitment? Are you committed to fidelity? Are you committed to marital growth? What are the distinctive marks that set your marriage apart as a Christian marriage? Is it the loving way you relate to one another? Do the words "creativity" and "service" describe aspects of your marriage?

So many times as we search for deeper spiritual truths dealing with marriage, we return to our mentors, David and Vera Mace. And from our own personal observations, the words "creativity" and "service" describe David and Vera Mace. When others their age were retiring and rocking on their porches, they continued—well into their eighties—to speak and train couples in marriage enrichment. And as a widow at ninety-two, Vera coauthored a paper with us for the United Nation's International Year of the Family. She is an amazing lady, and we will always be grateful for what she and David have meant to us.

In their book *What's Happening to Clergy Marriages?* the Maces share their core beliefs. These five beliefs, if adopted (and acted upon), could form the sacred canopy for your marriage!

1. We believe that it was God who brought us together in the first place.
2. We believe that our continuing life together is part of the divine purpose.

3. We believe that we have a witness to bear together.
4. We believe that our shared life must have a sacrificial quality.
5. We believe that our Christian marriage must find spiritual expression.[4]

We challenge you to build a sacred canopy over your marriage. Then you can have a marriage that is truly Christian. Our faith in God, and our beliefs about Christian marriage, should make a radical difference in our relationship with our spouse.

OPEN YOUR HEART

In *To Understand Each Other*, Dr. Tournier wrote,

> God is passionately interested in each human being. To receive God is also, therefore, to receive his intense interest for those with whom we have rubbed shoulders without really seeming to understand them. [This could be your mate!] It is impossible to open one's heart to God without also opening it to one's fellow.[5]

It is God who can open your eyes and heart and give you a new passion for your mate and help you build a sacred canopy for your marriage. He can give you a new passion to understand your spouse. "As soon as a person feels understood," Tournier continues, "he opens up, and because he lowers his defenses, he is also able to make himself better understood."[6]

RELATIONSHIP IS THE KEY!

To have a truly Christian marriage, couples must have an open, honest relationship with each other. Couples who are able to construct their own sacred marriage canopy, surmount this eighth midlife challenge (as well as the other seven), and build a companionship marriage can be to others a living example of an enriched Christian marriage.

A friend challenged us: "Wait a minute. I like the idea of the sacred marriage canopy and having a more egalitarian, companionship

> Give group members a few moments to answer. If responses are lagging, ask questions like, How many of you have devotions together? Ask the ones who respond positively to share when they do their devotions, where they do them, and what resources they have used.

ONE ON ONE (10 minutes)

Please turn to pages 294 through 296. There you will find the three basic suggestions we referred to earlier, along with some questions for you to answer. While it's good to spend time on the first two suggestions, focus most of your discussion on the third item, "Together serve others." Brainstorm areas of ministry in which the two of you can serve together.

> After 9 minutes give your group a 1-minute warning before moving on to the next segment.

WRAP-UP (5 minutes)

Well, we have made it through the eight challenges. The first challenge asked us to let go of past marital disappointments, forgive each other, and commit to making the rest of our marriage the best. The second challenge was to create a partner-focused rather than a child-focused marriage. Maintaining an effective communication system that allows each person to express deep feelings, joys, and concerns was the third challenge. Using anger and conflict to build a stronger relationship was challenge number four. Challenges five and six were somewhat related: build a deeper friendship and enjoy your spouse, as well as renew romance and restore a pleasurable sexual relationship with your spouse. The seventh challenge took a look at our relationship with our aging parents and our adult children.

Finally, in this session we examined the eighth challenge, which dealt with the spiritual aspect of our relationship. And to help you along your way, I recommend you work through the Marriage Builder found on page 184.

Though we're out of challenges, we still have one more session to go. Dave and Claudia introduce us to John and Sarah McCracken. Read through their story, which begins on page 187, for they are a couple "who in midlife had the courage and confidence to make needed changes to grow in their personal life and in their marriage relationship."

Then read part 4, "The Marriage Challenge," which begins on page 207.

Meet John and Sarah McCracken

———— ————

There is no possible doubt that we can have better marriages if we want them enough.

—David and Vera Mace[1]

We want to introduce you to a couple who in midlife had the courage and confidence to make needed changes to grow in their personal life and in their marriage relationship. They are a living example that marital growth can take place at any point of a marriage—even one that has been in neutral for many years.

We met John and Sarah McCracken almost twenty years ago, when they were in their forties and in the middle of parenting adolescents. We still remember the first time we were invited to their house for dinner. When our son, Jonathan, spilled his spaghetti on one of their lovely upholstered dining room chairs, they handled his accident with grace and humor. Here was a family we wanted to know better. The McCrackens were creative and fun to be with. Over the years, we developed a deep and abiding friendship with their whole family.

John is a surgeon. Sarah was a full-time mom. Their three children were creative, independent, and completely different from each other. The first half of the McCrackens' marriage went according to plan. John worked hard and provided abundantly for his family while keeping up his golfing skills. Sarah enjoyed the challenge of providing the environment for growth for her children, and participated in book

187

PART FOUR

The Marriage Challenge

———— ————

Then, whatever weather come, or shine, or shade,
We'll set out together, not a whit afraid.
Age is ne'er alarming—I shall find, I ween,
You at sixty charming as at sweet sixteen.

—D. M. M. Craik

ONE ON ONE

Read over the following suggestions for continuing on your spiritual journey together. Discuss the questions that go with each suggestion, focusing most of your discussion time on the third suggestion, "Together serve others."

1. Accept where both you and your spouse are on your spiritual journey.

- Don't force or coerce your spouse to attend or do something with you that you know he or she will not enjoy.
- Be teachable and willing to learn.
- Realize that one of the privileges and joys of a marriage is having to relate one to one.

Do you agree fundamentally with each other on spiritual matters?

Do you see yourself and your spouse as being teachable and willing to learn?

Can you agree on more than you disagree on?

2. Promote spiritual closeness and unity through dialogue, devotions, and/or prayer together. If you would like to develop the habit of praying together, invest 10 minutes a day.

- Try the 10-minute miracle:

Scripture reading (5 minutes)
One prays (2 minutes)
The other prays (2 minutes)
Silence before the Lord (1 minute)
Monday, Wednesday, Friday the husband leads
Tuesday, Thursday, Saturday the wife leads
Sunday the Lord leads

What do you do as a couple to promote spiritual closeness?

Would the 10-minute miracle work for you?

When would be the best time for you to get together as a couple and share a devotion together or pray together?

3. Together serve others.

- The Lord is the one who gives purpose and meaning to our marriage.
- Reflect his image together in a hurting world.

- Be beacons that give light to others and create a thirst for healthy marriage relationships.

What is something about which we are both passionate?

How do we want others to perceive our marriage?

If we have adult children (or will have), how can we be role models for them?

What are some ways in which we can serve others together?

Also, you may want to start thinking about what you would like to do, after this study is concluded, to keep growing in your marriage. Next time I will introduce you to another video curriculum that Dave and Claudia have put together called *10 Great Dates*, which might be a good follow-up to this study.

Close in Prayer

Dear Father, we desire our marriage to be the best it can be. We want it to glorify you. Help us to grow closer to you and closer to one another. Give us hearts that accept each other and build one another up. And Lord, please help our marriages to be a beacon of light to other couples—to be model of your love and reflect your image. Amen.

Planning Notes

_____

_____

_____

_____

_____

_____

_____

_____

_____

_____

_____

_____

_____

_____

_____

_____

_____

_____

_____

_____

_____

_____

_____

_____

_____

_____

_____

_____

_____

_____

_____

_____

_____

_____

_____

_____

_____

_____

_____

_____

_____

Session 10: The Story of the McCrackens, and the Marriage Challenge

LEADER PREPARATION

Meet John and Sarah McCracken

In part 3 Claudia and Dave introduce us to John and Sarah McCracken, "who have lived through this process and met the challenges remarkably well ... as they transitioned from raising three children to facing the empty nest and on to enjoying retirement.... [They] had the courage and confidence to make needed changes to grow in their personal life and in their marriage relationship. They are a living example that marital growth can take place at any point of a marriage—even one that has been in neutral for many years."

During the first half of the McCrackens' marriage, both worked hard, John as a surgeon, Sarah as a full-time mom and community leader. Both were content with their traditional roles. But when the children began leaving home, the second half of John and Sarah's marriage wasn't so smooth. They were virtually "unprepared for the changes and challenges ahead of them."

John said that he prided himself on his role as provider and on how he was esteemed in the medical community. His focus was his work and accomplishments. However, as they were approaching the empty nest, a family vacation to Europe changed his perspective. He felt like an outsider in his own family, while he viewed Sarah as having a much closer relationship to their children.

John wondered how he had lost touch with his family. He felt alone and unappreciated. When John tried to reconnect with Sarah, it made her uncomfortable. For the first twenty-five years of marriage, they had a comfortable, albeit distant, relationship. While they didn't have a lot of closeness, Sarah considered their marriage above average. As they transitioned into the empty nest, this sudden change in John was scary for Sarah.

Sarah said, "I am a very intense person, extremely interested in the world around me; I needed something to pour my energy into. I never gave much consideration to pouring that energy into my marriage."

Eventually they both decided to focus on their marriage. Sarah said, "One of the first things we discovered was that the second half of marriage is a very personal stage of life, and neither of us handled the personal side of life very well." Nevertheless, John and Sarah decided to work on their relationship, knowing it would be costly emotionally.

Planning Notes

_____
_____
_____
_____
_____
_____
_____
_____
_____
_____
_____
_____
_____
_____
_____
_____
_____
_____
_____
_____
_____
_____
_____
_____
_____
_____
_____
_____
_____
_____
_____
_____
_____
_____
_____

They discovered that their communication and intimacy needed some help. "It wasn't that we disagreed more than other couples. It was more as if we lived parallel lives with separate goals, concerns, hopes, and joys."

To remedy this, they agreed to make themselves more vulnerable with each other and express their inner feelings. They needed to reexamine their roles and how decisions were made. Sarah said, "First, we both had to give up a little of our individuality and independence to forge a companionship marriage. Second, it was going to cost us time and energy, and later when we chose a common project to learn how to work together, it was going to cost us financially!"

One of the many things they did to improve their marriage was to define their passions and interests. In comparing their lists, they discovered that they were on two different tracts. Nonetheless, they decided to focus on things they had in common. They also decided to forge ahead into unknown territory together. They decided to build a mountain home.

John said, "At this point, we began cutting loose of some of the things that had gripped us in the past. We began to experiment and try new things. But the really positive thing was that we were doing it together! At last we were learning to cooperate and work together."

Their building project helped bring them closer together and appreciate each other as individuals. They also decided to put some fun into their marriage. John said, "Developing shared interests has not been a snap for us. It took time and real commitment. But it has been a key element in making our marriage better."

Challenge Your Marriage

Dave and Claudia challenge us to think about our marriage. What changes have occurred in the last decade? What changes do you want to make in the future? They write, "Psychologists tell us it takes three weeks to make a new habit, and six weeks to feel comfortable about it. As we work with couples, so many times we see that it's not a matter of knowing what to do but doing what we know. It is up to you to define what you are going to do in the next weeks, months, and years to enrich your marriage and move it from better to best."

WELCOME (1 minute)

Call your group together and welcome them to the last session of this series. You will be discussing the last two parts of the book. Let your class know how much you've enjoyed the series, and encourage them to set some goals to help them keep growing in their marriage.

Planning Notes

OPEN IN PRAYER (1 minute)

Lord God, we have looked at eight marital challenges that face us during the empty nest years. And today we're going to take a look at another couple's journey. As each couple here makes decisions in the days, weeks, months, and years to follow, help us to work toward loving each other more and building a true companionship marriage. Also, lead us to other couples who we can help on their journey. Amen.

REVIEW SESSION NINE (1 minute)

During our last time together we defined the term "sacred canopy of protection over marriage." We also discussed ways in which we could help each other and ourselves in our spiritual pilgrimage.

OVERVIEW OF SESSION TEN (1 minute)

Please turn to page 299. Today we are going to explore:

- How John and Sarah McCracken reinvented their marriage as they transitioned into the empty nest years
- How we want to challenge our own marital growth in the second half of life
- Setting marriage goals for the future

MARRIAGE FORUM (10 minutes)

There is no video clip for today's session. Instead let me recap for you what John and Sarah McCracken shared in part 3. If you turn to page 300, you can follow the key points of their story.

1. The first half of the McCrackens' marriage was busy, productive, and the "typical, traditional marriage."
2. With children leaving home, Sarah felt as if she were "out of a job," and John felt disconnected from Sarah.
3. They discovered that the second half of marriage is a very personal stage of life. They also discovered that having a good second half is a choice.
4. They learned that building a good second half relationship is costly in terms of time, energy, and even money.
5. In order to develop a closer relationship, they had to become vulnerable to each other and disclose inner feelings.

Planning Notes

_____

_____

_____

_____

_____

_____

_____

_____

_____

_____

_____

_____

_____

_____

_____

_____

_____

_____

_____

_____

_____

_____

_____

_____

_____

_____

_____

_____

_____

_____

_____

_____

_____

_____

_____

_____

Session 10

_____ ✴ _____

THE STORY OF THE MCCRACKENS, AND THE MARRIAGE CHALLENGE

OVERVIEW OF THIS SESSION

Today we are going to explore:

- How John and Sarah McCracken reinvented their marriage as they transitioned into the empty nest years

- How we want to challenge our own marital growth in the second half of life

- Setting marriage goals for the future

_____ ✴ _____

299

MARRIAGE FORUM

1. The first half of the McCrackens' marriage was busy, productive, and the "typical, traditional marriage."

2. With children leaving home, Sarah felt as if she were "out of a job," and John felt disconnected from the family.

3. They discovered that the second half of marriage is a very personal stage of life. They also discovered that having a good second half is a choice.

4. They learned that building a good second half relationship is costly in terms of time, energy, and even money.

5. In order to develop a closer relationship, they had to become vulnerable to each other and disclose inner feelings.

6. They discovered that they had to give up a little of their individuality and independence in order to create a companionship marriage.

7. They reviewed their individual interests and passions, compared notes, and came up with interests they had in common.

8. Realizing that former activities could be detrimental to their second half of marriage, they forged ahead and agreed to try new things. They looked for ways to instill some fun into their marriage.

MY REFLECTION TIME

Working individually, complete the section labeled "Mine" in the following chart.

6. They discovered that they had to give up a little of their individuality and independence in order to create a companionship marriage.

7. They reviewed their individual interests and passions, compared notes, and came up with interests they had in common or together could develop.

8. Realizing that former activities could be detrimental to their second half of marriage, they forged ahead and agreed to try new things. They looked for ways to instill some fun into their marriage.

As you look over these eight points, which ones do you identify with?

> Allow time for participants to respond. If response is slow, try asking questions like, How many of you can identify with item 1? How would you describe a "typical, traditional marriage"?

How could building a closer relationship in the empty nest years be costly? What kinds of energy sacrifices might you have to make?

> Allow time for participants to respond.

As you read through the McCrackens' story, what thoughts, feelings, or even fears did you have? Was there anything especially encouraging, inspiring, or motivating for you?

> Allow time for participants to respond.

MY REFLECTION TIME (8 minutes)

Please look at pages 300 and 301. One of the things the McCrackens did was to explore their individual interests and passions and then come up with a list of things they had in common. For the next 10 minutes I want you to work as individuals. Look at the categories in the "Interests and Passions Chart" provided . Note that there are three categories: "Mine," "My Spouse's," "Ours." Complete the section labeled "Mine" for now.

> After 7 minutes have elapsed, give the group a 1-minute warning before asking them to start comparing their lists.

Planning Notes

_____

_____

_____

_____

_____

_____

_____

_____

_____

_____

_____

_____

_____

_____

_____

_____

_____

_____

_____

_____

_____

_____

_____

_____

_____

_____

_____

_____

_____

_____

_____

_____

_____

_____

_____

_____

_____

---

300 ❧ *The Second Half of Marriage Participant's Guide*

MARRIAGE FORUM

1. The first half of the McCrackens' marriage was busy, productive, and the "typical, traditional marriage."

2. With children leaving home, Sarah felt as if she were "out of a job," and John felt disconnected from the family.

3. They discovered that the second half of marriage is a very personal stage of life. They also discovered that having a good second half is a choice.

4. They learned that building a good second half relationship is costly in terms of time, energy, and even money.

5. In order to develop a closer relationship, they had to become vulnerable to each other and disclose inner feelings.

6. They discovered that they had to give up a little of their individuality and independence in order to create a companionship marriage.

7. They reviewed their individual interests and passions, compared notes, and came up with interests they had in common.

8. Realizing that former activities could be detrimental to their second half of marriage, they forged ahead and agreed to try new things. They looked for ways to instill some fun into their marriage.

MY REFLECTION TIME

Working individually, complete the section labeled "Mine" in the following chart.

Session 10 ❧ 301

Interests and Passions Chart			
Category	Mine	My Spouse's	Ours
Church			
Home			
Travel			
Family Activities			
Sports and Recreation			
Reading			
Entertainment			
Possible "Couple Project"			

ONE ON ONE

Compare notes with your spouse. In the section marked "My Spouse's," list the things your spouse put on his or her list.

Compare notes again and write the activities you share in common in the "Ours" column.

MARRIAGE FORUM

Did you have more interests and passions in common with your spouse or more that were different?

Were you surprised by something your spouse listed?

Did you not have anything in common in any category?

ONE ON ONE (8 minutes)

In a moment I want you to compare your notes. In the section marked "My Spouse's," list the things your spouse put on his or her list.

Next the fun part starts as you compare notes again and write the activities you share in common in the "Ours" column.

Please break into your one-on-one groups now.

> After 7 minutes have elapsed, give the group a 1-minute warning before continuing on to the next segment.

MARRIAGE FORUM (5 minutes)

Please turn to pages 301–302. You may stay where you are for the next section. Let's discuss what you discovered. How many couples found they had more in common than they had differences?

> Ask for a show of hands.

How many of you were surprised by something your spouse listed?

> Ask for a show of hands.

Did anyone not have anything in common in any category?

> Ask for a show of hands.

How many of you believe you could take what's listed in your "Our" column and begin building a closer relationship?

> Ask for a show of hands.

Are there any comments you would like to share regarding this exercise? Was it helpful? Revealing? Encouraging?

> Allow a few moments for people to respond.

Planning Notes

_____
_____
_____
_____
_____
_____
_____
_____
_____
_____
_____
_____
_____
_____
_____
_____
_____
_____
_____
_____
_____
_____
_____
_____
_____
_____
_____
_____
_____
_____
_____
_____

Session 10 ✖ 301

Interests and Passions Chart

Category	Mine	My Spouse's	Ours
Church			
Home			
Travel			
Family Activities			
Sports and Recreation			
Reading			
Entertainment			
Possible "Couple Project"			

ONE ON ONE

Compare notes with your spouse. In the section marked "My Spouse's," list the things your spouse put on his or her list.

Compare notes again and write the activities you share in common in the "Ours" column.

MARRIAGE FORUM

Did you have more interests and passions in common with your spouse or more that were different?

Were you surprised by something your spouse listed?

Did you not have anything in common in any category?

---

302 ✖ *The Second Half of Marriage Participant's Guide*

Do you believe you could take what's listed in your "Our" column and begin building a closer relationship?

Was this exercise helpful? Revealing? Encouraging?

ONE ON ONE

Please turn to page 214. The Marriage Builder there is based on the eight challenges couples face during the second half of marriage. Take the next 10 minutes and go through each challenge, evaluating:

1. Your growth in this area
2. Where you still need to grow
3. What you can do, individually and as a couple, to meet the challenge

WRAP-UP

We will review the materials in this study on the following date:

ONE ON ONE (10 minutes)

At the end of our last session I recapped for you the eight challenges couples face during the second half of marriage. Please turn to page 214. There you will find a Marriage Builder that will help you evaluate your marriage against the backdrop of the eight challenges we have discussed. Take the next ten minutes and go through each challenge on page 302, evaluating:

1. Your growth in this area
2. Where you still need to grow
3. What you can do, individually and as a couple, to meet the challenge

You may not get through all eight challenges during this discussion time, but that's okay. I hope you will continue this discussion this week—and in the weeks, months, and years to follow.

> After 9 minutes have elapsed, give your group a 1-minute warning before going on to the final segment.

WRAP-UP (15 minutes)

I hope that the last ten sessions have brought each of you closer together as couples. I hope you feel encouraged and motivated to "make the rest the best," as the Arps would say.

As we come to the end of this study, would anyone like to share what you have learned? What new things do you plan to implement in your marriage?

> Allow time for people to respond.

The most important part of this study is what you do now to keep your relationship alive and growing. Remember the Arps' challenge to build your friendship and to have fun dates. You might want to work through their book *10 Great Dates* (Zondervan), or you may want to continue this group and go through the *10 Great Dates* video curriculum. You could invite other couples of any age and stage of marriage to join the group. The format of the *10 Great Dates* study is simple. After watching a short "video date launch," each couple actually goes on a date. Some groups enjoy getting back together after each date for dessert and discussion. Let me show you a brief 3-minute video clip that introduces this program.

Planning Notes

_____

_____

_____

_____

_____

_____

_____

_____

_____

_____

_____

_____

_____

_____

_____

_____

_____

_____

_____

_____

_____

_____

_____

_____

_____

_____

_____

_____

_____

_____

214　❧　The Second Half of Marriage

———————— ❧ ————————

MARRIAGE BUILDER

Challenging Your Marriage

Our challenge to you is to discuss the eight marital challenges. You can use the following three questions to kick off your discussion. You goal is to evaluate where you are, where you would like to be, and what steps you need to take too improve your relationship in each of the eight areas. The three questions are:

1. What evidence is there that we are growing in this area?
2. What evidence is there that we still need to grow in this area?
3. What can I personally do to help us meet this challenge?

The eight marital challenges for the second half of marriage are:

1. Let go of past marital disappointments, forgive each other, and commit to making the rest of your marriage the best.
2. Create a marriage that is partner-focused rather than child-focused.
3. Maintain an effective communication system that allows you to express your deepest feelings, joys, and concerns.
4. Use anger and conflict in a creative way to build your relationship.
5. Build a deeper friendship and enjoy your spouse.
6. Renew romance and restore a pleasurable sexual relationship.
7. Adjust to changing roles with aging parents and adult children.
8. Evaluate where you are on your spiritual pilgrimage, grow closer to each other and to God, and together serve others.

302　❧　The Second Half of Marriage Participant's Guide

Do you believe you could take what's listed in your "Our" column and begin building a closer relationship?

Was this exercise helpful? Revealing? Encouraging?

ONE ON ONE

Please turn to page 214. The Marriage Builder there is based on the eight challenges couples face during the second half of marriage. Take the next 10 minutes and go through each challenge, evaluating:

1. Your growth in this area
2. Where you still need to grow
3. What you can do, individually and as a couple, to meet the challenge

WRAP-UP

We will review the materials in this study on the following date:

Optional: Show the *10 Great Dates* preview video and discuss whether the group might like to start a *10 Great Dates* group. Give couples an opportunity to indicate if they are interested. Perhaps one couple would volunteer to facilitate the group. It's even easier to lead than this study! As the leader of this group, you may want to facilitate it.

Allow time for people to respond and discuss the possibilities of continuing.

Let me encourage you to stay in touch with each other. Perhaps there is a couple or several couples from within this group who would enjoy developing friendships and encouraging one another to keep working on their marriages. Especially as situations come up with aging parents or grown children, it's good to have a support group handy.

As this is our last session together, there is no particular assignment other than to review the material every so often. Perhaps a six-month checkup would be in order. Make it a getaway weekend for the two of you to go back through the material and chart your progress. In fact, on page 302 there is a space where you can write in a date when you will review what you have learned. I encourage you to fill it in, place a reminder on your planning calendar, and do it!

Close in Prayer

Father, we have come to the end of this series but to the beginning of a new life together. Help us to apply to our marriage the principles and skills we have learned over the last ten sessions. Guide us as we build a companionship marriage, as we dedicate ourselves to serving others, and as we strive to make the rest the best. Amen.

Note: If you don't include the *10 Great Dates* preview clip as part of the last session, arrange for those interested to view it after the session or at another time. The clip is the last few minutes of video 2.

Planning Notes

_____

_____

_____

_____

_____

_____

_____

_____

_____

_____

_____

_____

_____

_____

_____

_____

_____

_____

_____

_____

_____

_____

_____

_____

_____

_____

_____

_____

_____

_____

_____

_____

_____

_____

About the Authors

Claudia Arp and David Arp, MSW, are founders and directors of Marriage Alive International, Inc., a marriage and family ministry offering a full range of resources including seminars, curriculum, training, and consulting. They conduct seminars across the United States and Europe, and are frequent contributors to print and broadcast media. They have appeared as empty nest experts on the NBC *Today Show* and *CBS This Morning*, and host their own syndicated radio program, *The Family Workshop*, heard daily on over 200 stations. They are columnists, with several magazines including *Marriage* magazine and *Christian Parenting Today*.

The Arps have written numerous books, including *10 Great Dates, Suddenly They're 13*, and *Fighting for Your Empty Nest Marriage*, which they coauthored with martial researchers Howard Markman, Scott Stanley, and Susan Blumberg, developers of the acclaimed Prevention and Relationship Enhancement Program (PREP). Their credentials include over 25 years as marriage and family educators and their 37-year, rock-solid marriage—including 10 years in their own empty nest so they have personally experienced what they talk about in this video curriculum. The Arps have three adult sons and five grandchildren and live in Knoxville, Tennessee.

About the Writer

Sharon Lamson is a freelance writer/editor with a diverse writing background. She has produced newsletters, brochures, and other marketing literature for various companies and nonprofit organizations across the country. In addition, Sharon has written both classroom and online curriculum for a scouting-type organization that services children with disabilities.

She has also coauthored three adventure books for children (*The Barn at Gun Lake*, *Mystery Explosion*, and *Discovery on Blackbird Island*, published by Cedar Tree Publishing).

Besides writing for children, Sharon has developed Sunday school curriculum for adults based on the book *Relationships* by Drs. Les and Leslie Parrott (Zondervan, 1999).

Sharon enjoys speaking, drama, and keeping up with her four active teenagers. She and her husband, Robert, currently live in Norton Shores, Michigan.

RESOURCES BY DAVID & CLAUDIA ARP

BOOKS

10 Great Dates

The Second Half of Marriage

Fighting for Your Empty Nest Marriage (coauthors with Scott Stanley,
   Howard Markman & Susan Blumberg)

Marriage Devotional Bible (coauthors with Les & Leslie Parrott and Bob
and Rosemary Barnes)

Love Life for Parents

Suddenly They're 13

52 Dates for You and Your Mate

Marriage Moments

Family Moments

Quiet Whispers from God's Heart for Couples

The Big Book of Family Fun (coauthored with Linda Dillow)

The Ultimate Marriage Builder

Where the Wild Strawberries Grow

VIDEO KITS

10 Great Dates to Energize Your Marriage

The Second Half of Marriage

PEP Groups for Parents of Teens

PEP Groups for Moms

Moms' & Dads' Support Group

For more information about these and other Marriage Alive Resources contact:

Marriage Alive International, Inc
10028 Quarry Hill Place
Denver, CO 80134
Phone: 303.840.1518
Resource Line: 1.888.690.6667
E-mail: mailine97@aol.com
www.marriagealive.com

To receive the Arps free weekly Marriage Builder e-mail newsletter, send the message "subscribe zphlove" (without quotation marks) to: lists@info.harpercollins.com

Ten Fun-Filled Couples' Nights Out ™
That Will Energize Your Marriage!

10 Great Dates to Energize Your Marriage

David and Claudia Arp

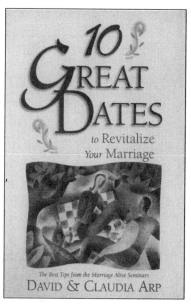

Dating doesn't have to be only a memory or just another boring evening at the movies. David and Claudia Arp have revolutionized dating by creating Couples' Nights Out ™ —memory-making evenings built on key, marriage-enriching themes. This approach to relationship growth involves both partners, is low-key, and most of all, is exciting, proven, and FUN!

Drawing upon the best tips from David and Claudia Arp's popular Marriage Alive Seminars in this book, *10 Great Dates*, you'll learn how to:

- Communicate better
- Build a creative sex life
- Process anger and resolve conflicts
- Develop spiritual intimacy
- Balance busy lifestyles
- And more!

Softcover 0-310-21091-7

Also Look For...

10 Great Dates to Energize Your Marriage Video Curriculum

This video curriculum is based on the Marriage Alive Seminars and the *10 Great Dates to Energize Your Marriage* book.

The Curriculum Kit contains:
- Two 75-minute videos with ten short date launches
- One *10 Great Dates to Energize Your Marriage* softcover (208 pages)
- One Leader's Guide (48 pages)

ISBN 0-310-21350-9

> *"The Arps are sure to revive romance and rejuvenate the fun quotient in your marriage!"*

> \- Drs. Les & Leslie Parrott, authors of
> *Saving Your Marriage Before It Starts*

Marriage Devotional Bible
NIV

David and Claudia Arp, Robert and Rosemary Barnes, and Les and Leslie Parrott

The *Marriage Devotional Bible* with the NIV helps couples maintain or rekindle the kind of rich, loving union God intended for them. Whether they've been married fewer than five years, are in the child-rearing stage, or in the years of mature love, every married couple will gain a greater closeness to each other as they bring the riches of God's truth into their relationship. Combining the marital counsel of acclaimed Christian marriage authors David and Claudia Arp, Robert and Rosemary Barnes, and Les and Leslie Parrott, the *Marriage Devotional Bible* offers enriching features such as:

- Building Our Marriage: 260 daily devotions tied to Scripture passages that help a married couple understand God's design for marriage and give practical insights into achieving his ideal.
- Quiet Times with Each Other: 52 weekly devotions encourage couples to take a step back, evaluate their union, and enjoy God's presence together.
- Just Between You and Me: 60 marriage checkups help reveal the needs of each partner, allowing them to discuss issues before they begin to hinder intimacy with God and each other.
- Couples of the Bible: Profiles both good and bad examples of married couples. This feature offers readers points of discussion and application to improve their relationship with God and their spouse.
- Legacy pages: Couples can record significant moments in their relationship that they can share with their family and friends.

By using this devotional Bible, couples can incorporate the truth of God's Word into their relationship, infusing their marriage with God's love and inviting Christ's presence into every season of their lives together.

Pick up a copy today at your local bookstore!

Hardcover 0-310-90133-2
Softcover 0-310-90878-7
Burgundy Bonded Leather 0-310-91120-6

ZondervanPublishingHouse
Grand Rapids, Michigan
A Division of HarperCollinsPublishers

Reclaim the Passion That Got You Your Job as Parents in the First Place!

Love Life for Parents

How to Have Kids and a Sex Life Too

David and Claudia Arp

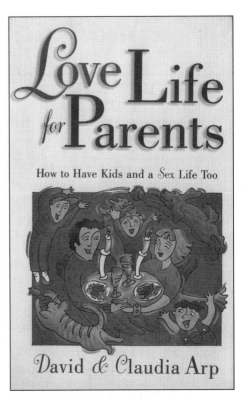

After a hectic day parenting children—no matter what their ages—few parents have enough energy and desire left for sex. Don't despair, help is here!

Love Life for Parents is an easy, fun, and realistic approach to putting interest back in intimacy, readiness back in romance, and the sizzle back in sex!

Whether you have just 60 seconds or 60 minutes, you'll find quick tips, frank advice, and one-of-a-kind ideas to teach the heart of every parent who wants to be a better lover.

Softcover 0-310-20715-0
Audio 0-310-21957-4

"Love Life for Parents is the Arps at their very best, offering practical advice, gentle humor, and wisdom they can only have acquired with time, patience, and practicing what they preach!"

-Liz Curtis Higgs,
Author, *Bad Girls of the Bible*

"What a great book! Explicit enough to be understandable, objective enough to be helpful, and readable enough to be entertaining . . . a must for every couple with kids."

-Bob and Rosemary Barnes,
Authors, *Great Sexpectations*

ZondervanPublishingHouse
Grand Rapids, Michigan

A Division of HarperCollinsPublishers

Suddenly They're 13

Or the Art of Hugging a Cactus

David and Claudia Arp

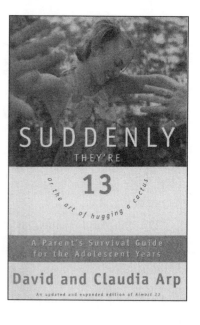

What do you do when your huggable kid suddenly sprouts needles? Don't despair! Help is here. You can learn how to relate to your teenage "cactus" and get through the critical adolescent passage—relationship intact.

Go with David and Claudia as they take you through The "Four Rs" of Parenting Your "Cactus":

Regroup: Evaluate your relationship
Release: Design your own plan for letting go
Relate: Get off the lecture circuit
Relax: Trust God for what you don't see

An updated and expanded edition of the international best-seller, *Almost 13* (over 125,000 in print), *Suddenly They're 13* with discussion guide is an indispensable guide for parents to successfully manage the "prickly" adolescent years. David and Claudia Arp provide tools to help you launch your kids into adulthood.

Softcover 0-310-22788-7

Pick up a copy today at your local bookstore!

"What a positive and practical approach to parenting teens! I love the action steps for encouraging teenagers and preparing them for life in the adult world. The ideas will be easy to pass on to parents of teens at my church, and I'm better prepared for my own children to suddenly turn thirteen!"

-Doug Fields, Youth Pastor, Saddleback Church;
Author, *Purpose-Driven Youth Ministry*

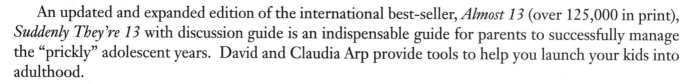

ZondervanPublishingHouse
Grand Rapids, Michigan

A Division of HarperCollinsPublishers

COUPLE ENRICHMENT
R E S O U R C E

About Marriage Alive
International, Inc.

Bringing marriages and families to life!

Marriage Alive is a groundbreaking church- and community-focused ministry offering a full range of marriage and family resources including seminars, curriculum, training, and consulting.

Our Vision is to see a movement of trained and equipped couples working through congregations and other established communities to transform marriage and family relationships.

Our Mission is to identify, train, and empower leaders who invest in others by building strong marriage and family relationships through the integration of biblical truth, contemporary research, practical application, and fun.

Our Strategy is to

- Develop community awareness through our resources, web site, media, conferences, and e-mail newsletters.
- Provide education through seminars, curriculum development, and cooperative learning.
- Train couples in leadership development through institutes and facilitator trainings.
- Mentor couples through couple-to-couple relationships and small group retreats, who will, in turn, invest in the lives of others.

Our Resources and Services

Marriage and family books in seven languages
Video-based educational programs
Nationally syndicated radio program, *The Family Workshop*
Marriage and family Seminars
Consulting, training, leadership development, and mentoring
Award-winning web site www.marriagealive.com

You can contact Marriage Alive at:

10028 Quarry Hill Place
Denver, CO 80134
Phone: 303.840.1518
Resource Line: 1.888.690.6667
E-mail: mailine97@aol.com

Seminars for Building Better Relationships

Suddenly They're 13

In this lively seminar, the Arps share the secrets for surviving the adolescent years. Learn how to regroup, release, relate, and relax! You can foster positive family dynamics, add fun and focus to your family and build supportive relationships with other parents. This seminar will help you prepare for the teenage years and then actually enjoy them. It's a great way to launch a PEP Group for Parents of Teen.

Marriage Alive

The Arps' most requested seminar is an exciting, fun-filled approach to building thriving marriages. Some of the topics included in this six-hour seminar are prioritizing you marriage, finding unity in diversity, communicating your feelings, processing anger and resolving conflict, cultivating spiritual intimacy, and having an intentional marriage.

The Second Half of Marriage

After the adolescent years comes the empty nest. Let the Arps help you prepare for it. Based on their national survey of long-term marriages and their Gold Medallion Award-winning book, *The Second Half of Marriage*, the Arps reveal eight challenges that all long-term marriages face and give practical strategies for surmounting each. Topics include choosing a partner-focused marriage, renewing the couple friendship, focusing on the future, and growing together spiritually.

Fun in Marriage Is Serious Business—A lighthearted presentation in which Dave and Claudia talk about the importance of building the couple friendship and putting more fun in marriage through dating. This high-energy presentation can be crafted to fit your time slot from a 30-minute, after-dinner talk to a whole evening of fun. This is a great way to kick off the 10 Great Dates program in your church or group.

To schedule the Arps for a seminar or other speaking engagement contact:

Alive Communications, Inc.
7680 Goddard Street
Suite 200,
Colorado Springs, CO 80920

Praise for *The Second Half of Marriage*

"No matter what challenges you previously faced, this resource can help you reinvent your marriage and renew your love for each other. Great for all who want to make the rest of their marriage the best!"

Timothy Clinton, Ph.D.,
president, American Association of Christian Counselors

"The Second Half of Marriage is full of rich insights into marriage in later life and the many challenges and hopes it offers. There is great wisdom in this volume in a vital area of life that is too often ignored. It is a must read."

John Gottman, Ph.D.,
marital researcher and author of
Why Marriages Succeed or Fail

"This should be required reading for every couple in the 'second half.' We highly recommend this resource in our mentoring program."

Drs. Les & Leslie Parrott,
co-directors of the Center for
Relationship Development, Seattle Pacific University
and authors of *Saving Your Marriage Before It Starts*

"We people of our proud, youth-oriented America tend to arrive at the maturing years of marriage with rusty relationships. The Arps' stiff scouring brush is a powerful anti-corrosive for 'Help, we're hitting bottom!' mid-lifers."

Howard and Jeanne Hendricks,
Distinguished Professor and Chairman
of the Center for Christian Leadership
Dallas Theological Seminary

We want to hear from you. Please send your comments about this
book to us in care of the address below. Thank you.

ZondervanPublishingHouse
Grand Rapids, Michigan 49530
http://www.zondervan.com